WHISKY & SCOTLAND

A Practical and Spiritual Survey

by

NEIL M. GUNN

SOUVENIR PRESS

First published in 1935, by George Routledge & Sons, London

This edition copyright © 1977 by Souvenir Press and John W. M. Gunn and published 1977 by Souvenir Press (Educational & Academic) Ltd., 43 Great Russell Street, London WC1B 3PA and simultaneously in Canada by Methuen Publications, Agincourt, Ontario

The publisher acknowledges the financial assistance of The Scottish Arts Council in the production of this volume

ISBN 0 285 62279 x casebound
ISBN 0 285 62289 7 paperback

Printed in Great Britain by
J. W. Arrowsmith, Bristol, BS3 2NT

CONTENTS

PART ONE
IN THE BEGINNING

		PAGE
UISGEBEATHA	. . . .	3
EARLY HISTORY	. . . .	16
LATER HISTORY	. . . .	28

PART TWO
THE SPIRIT

THE FATED CELTS	. . . . . .	47
THE DESCENT	. . . .	56
WHY?	. . . .	63
THE TRADITION	. . . .	65
IN SCOTLAND	. . . .	70
NATIONALISM	. . . .	78
THE INTERNATIONAL CUP	. . . . . .	88
HIGHLANDS AND LOWLANDS	. . . . .	99
SCOTTISH NATIONALISM	. . . . . .	115

PART THREE
WHISKY

WHISKY	. . . .	125
BARLEY	. . . .	129
MALTING	. . . .	131
BREWING	. . . .	134
DISTILLING	. . . .	141
MATURING	. . . .	147
BLENDING	. . . .	162
SOME SINGLE WHISKIES	. . . . . .	178
AN ECONOMIC NOTE	. . . . . .	188

FOREWORD TO 1977 EDITION

Grapes may hang heavy with a sun-kissed succulence. The year may be marked down as vintage, and wines pronounced impudent, discreet, domineering, provocative, even noble—but vineyard owners in their châteaux are probably savouring another drink.

For a greater 'wine', embodying in it the tempest of thunder and the sweetness of innocence, daring in its controlled smoothness, has become the one drink a French hostess cannot afford to be without.

Naturally, I refer to whisky—a work of art which is always repeated, yet always unique. Its embracing, possessive, all-round quality is wooing topers from the fiery concoctions of Chile, the sauternes of Spain and the age-old grip of the grape.

In France, where whisky was almost unknown before the Second World War, imports have spiralled upwards and the Auld Alliance is celebrated with more whisky drinking than in any other country apart from America, where consumption now is more than the world drank in 1939.

The world's thirst for Scotch is Sahara-dry, and the whisky maturing in Scotland today is worth much more than the entire gold reserves of the Bank of England even *before* the economic and industrial crisis of the last few years.

It was James Hogg, the Etterick Shepherd, who said of his favourite whisky: 'If a body could just find oot the exac' proper proportion and quantity that ought to be drunk every day, and keep to that, I verily trow that he might leeve for ever, without dying at a', and that doctors and kirkyards would go oot o' fashion.'

His judgement on the merits of whisky is completely endorsed. Despite imitations, competition from legitimate whiskies such as Irish, rye and bourbon, Scotch is the most popular drink in the world, as truly international as that celebration of sweet parting, *Auld Lang Syne*.

Blends still dominate the boardrooms, but the clear malts are Scotland's classic whiskies, each as distinctive as a smile, and smooth as the shimmer of a leaping salmon. Yet, strange as it may seem today, it was as a medicine that whisky first achieved popularity among the Scots, being prescribed 'for the preservation of health, the prolongation of life, and for the relief of colic, dropsy, palsy and smallpox, as well as a host of other ailments.'

Single malts must be drunk with circumspection. Contrary to the old joke about the Highlander liking two things naked, one of them whisky, malts are best drunk with a little water to bring out the aroma and flavour.

It was once explained to me by a lover of Laphroaig, an Islay malt that rolls in on you like a sea haar, that these whiskies are like an orchestra. 'The Islay malts are heavy and sombre as cellos. Highland malts are violas, Lowland the discursive violin. . . .'

But what of the great whiskies? Smith's Glenlivet,

from the Minmore distillery on Speyside, lays proud claim to the title of *The* Glenlivet. Others, like Miltonduff-Glenlivet or Longmorn-Glenlivet, must use a hyphen, and the addition is used in the same way as Chambertin has been added to the burgundies of Gevrey, and Musigny to those of Chambolle.

From Dufftown, a capital of malt distilling—'Rome was built on seven hills, Dufftown stands on seven stills'—comes Glenfiddich, cream-smooth on the tongue, along with Mortlach. Glenfarclas-Glenlivet, a distilled dew created at Ballindalloch, has the insistent Tomintoul-Glenlivet as a companion. From Keith, also in Banffshire, comes gentle Strathisla, and from further west in Elgin thrive a duo that deserve wider fame—Linkwood and Longmorn. The list is endless—Glenmorangie, distilled in Tain, retains a heather-honey flavour. Balmore, from Invergordon, Glen-mhor at Inverness, Balblair discreet at Edderton in Ross-shire, Cardhu, pride of Knockandow, and Clynelish out of Brora, pure as a pibroch. In Skye there is the brooding Tallisker, powerful enough to suit any man's mood, and among the Islay malts there is the mellow supremacy of Lagavulin; and at Craigel-lachie there is the mighty Macallan which, it is said, was offered as an alternative to cognac at a Mansion House dinner in London in honour of Kruschev and Bulga-nin during their 1956 visit. In Orkney, there is the polished suaveness of Highland Park, and in Stirling-shire there is Glengoyne, a Lowland malt fit to start a Trossachs trek.

At the end of 1976 there were 1,100 million gallons (8,800 million bottles) in bond, enough to supply world markets for up to eight years even if demand grew at five percent a year, and almost half of this hip flask wealth is controlled by the mammoth Distillers Company, a combine which turns out five of the best-known blended labels in the business—Haig, Johnnie Walker, Black and White, White Horse and Dewar's White Label. Indeed, the group sells one out of every six bottles of Scotch consumed throughout the world.

But is the unparalleled commercial success of this century finally going to be sabotaged by successive Chancellors who keep on putting up taxation, and by governments who don't understand that Scotch—apart altogether from the bulk shipments of malt—is a unique product which needs protection? Equally disturbing is the continual harassment of the industry. Distillery companies, as distinct from brewers, have to pay excise duty *immediately* whisky is removed from bond, which means that on any day they are subsidising the Government to between £50 and £60 million, as it takes some eight months for companies to regain their money via sales. And at Christmas and New Year this penal subsidy rises to well over the £100 million mark.

Another point of discrimination is that even on alcoholic strength, the whisky drinker is penalised by tax more than three times as much as the beer drinker!

Neil Gunn, lover of words and whisky, and a long-time friend of my father, Hugh MacDiarmid, was equally bitter about the malevolent tax: 'The discrimination against whisky is so manifestly unjust that it does have the appearance of being deliberately vindictive. . . .'

He would be glad, however, that William Grant & Sons, distillers of Glenfiddich and Balvenie, as well as being blenders of Standfast, founded an Academy of Pure Malt Whisky in 1972 in response to the rapidly growing interest in malts. My father is one of the governors, and I have no doubt that Neil Gunn would have been one also if such an institution had existed when he was at the dramming, for single malts, with all their individuality, recalled to him:

'... The world of hills and glens, of raging elements, of shelter, of divine ease. The perfect moment of their reception is after bodily stress—or mental stress, if the body be sound. The essential oils that wind in the glass then uncurl their long fingers in lingering benediction and the whole works of creation are made manifest. At such a moment the basest man would bless his enemy.'

We would all stand and echo *Slainte!* to that sustained tribute, but Gunn, in his search for, and experience of, human values and experience also noted elsewhere: 'Man must for ever move like a liberator through his own unconsciousness.'

And whisky in *Whisky and Scotland*, the latest reprint of his works by Souvenir Press, is much more than an eloquent metaphor, as he observes at the book's end: 'And when I use the word whisky I can but hope that the reader who has followed this long and devious excursion may now have some faint glimmering of what I mean.'

MICHAEL GRIEVE

PART ONE
IN THE BEGINNING

UISGEBEATHA [1]

WHISKY comes from the Gaelic *uisge-beatha* meaning 'water of life.' In the curious mind this will at once rouse wonder, perhaps even a contemplative effort to surprise the ancestral thought in its creative moment. For clearly there is nothing haphazard or transitory about the designation. It was not coined for the slang or commerce of any age. Rather is it akin to one of the ultimate elements into which ancient philosophers resolved the universe. It is not a description so much as a simple statement of truth and of mystery.

Is it now possible to conceive by what process some long-dead mouth and tongue were led to breathe out the magic syllables upon the liquor's aftermath?

Down round the southern corner of the *dun* there was a field of barley all ripened by the sun. In a small wind it echoed faintly the sound of the ocean; at night it sighed and rustled as the earth mother thought over things, not without a little anxiety. It was cut and harvested and a sheaf offered in thanks-

---

[1] *Pron.* ooshkubeha (ooshku, *whence* whisky).

3

giving; flailed and winnowed; until the ears of grain remained in a heap of pale gold: the bread of life.

In simple ways the grain was prepared and ground and set to ferment; the fermented liquor was then boiled, and as the steam came off it was by happy chance condensed against some cold surface.

And lo! this condensation of the steam from the greenish-yellow fermented gruel is clear as crystal. It is purer than any water from any well. When cold, it is colder to the fingers than ice.

A marvellous transformation. A perfect water. But in the mouth—what is this? The gums tingle, the throat burns, down into the belly fire passes, and thence outward to the finger-tips, to the feet, and finally to the head.

The man was a bit tired, exasperated a little, for things had been going wrong (how often they must have gone wrong with the primitive experimenter!), and, for the rest—or he wouldn't have been at the job—not a little weary with the dulness of social life, including the looks of women and the ambitions of fools.

And then—and then—the head goes up. The film dissolves from the eyes; they glisten. He abruptly laughs and jumps to his feet; as abruptly pauses to look over himself with a marvelling scrutiny. He tries the muscles of his arms. They are full of such

4

energy that one fist shoots out; then the other. A right and left. His legs have the same energy. He begins to dance with what is called primitive abandon. Clearly it was not water he had drunk: *it was life.*

I know this is rather a poetic reconstruction, to be regarded with proper amusement, yet it is difficult to understand any history without some exercise of the imagination. What meaning can a human fact have until it is comprehended in thought and feeling? Let us pursue the method a little further.

Aware that he had achieved an 'epoch-making dis- covery,' his first impulse would be to communicate it to his friends. Again the cynical interpreter of history may doubt this; but here even recorded fact is with us overwhelmingly. For illicit distillation to-day, not only in the remote wastes of our mountains and glens but in our cities, could be carried on to a very great ex- tent without much fear of direct discovery by revenue officials, were it not that in one form or another 'information is received.' Sometimes this informa- tion is deliberately conveyed, more often it is over- heard. And even when deliberately conveyed, the motive is rarely or never one of pecuniary gain, but nearly always the satisfaction of some passion, thwarted or jealous or righteous. This might be illustrated with a recent instance which has come to my knowledge. Three men are standing at the public bar of an inn in one of the wildest and remotest places of Britain. They are drinking whisky, and having paid good money for it they are disposed to be critical. For it would appear they know better stuff than this. This stuff is watered to nothing and pretty rotten at that! They smile to each other knowingly. They wink. They ask the barman if this is the best he can do for them. Does he call this the real Mackay? They are a society getting fun out of their secret knowledge and urged to gloat over it by subtle innuendo. They give nothing directly away, of course. Indeed they would suffer any penalty rather than do that. But one traveller who is there, quietly having a drink by himself, overhears and wonders. He passes on the story and a few months later an illicit still is captured.

The first impulse, then, in the original discoverer would be to communicate with his friends. It is not impossible, however, that before actually setting off he tried his life-water again, just to make sure that he had not been a victim of some unusual form of witchery. It is even possible that as a scientist he considered it his duty to use his own body for further experimental purposes. While the poet would have arisen and gone singing through the forest at once, the scientist nobly prepares to sacrifice himself in the interests of knowledge.

6

Studying his reactions to a second draught, he would find that he had not been mistaken. Moreover, to the early ecstatic feelings there now supervened a state of consciousness marked by extreme mental clarity. Problems that had worried him for a long time, touching affairs of the family and the tribe, were seen in their true light, proportionately, and for what they were worth. And problems touching in particular the validity of certain religious aspects of totemic belief were seen to contain elements that were—peculiar. Decidedly peculiar. He smiled—to the liquor, which was of the ineffable transparency of truth. Another little test wouldn't do him any harm. . . . In this way, and as one of the first martyrs to science, he slowly ' passed out.'

But, like similar martyrs of a succeeding age, he would recover by-and-by, when, more than ever, he would desire to communicate with his friends, for what had been lost in initial eagerness would now be replaced with wisdom and a certain penetential awe.

His friends, his bosom cronies, would be more than taken in a little by this profound, even sad sense of experience, with its air of earnest secrecy. They had always said that one day he would go a bit too far; that some demon would possess him whom no druid could expel. Yet they liked him and so went privily with him through the woods to the small hill stream, taking care that neither Druid nor Chief saw them, and, in particular, that no scent of their intention crossed the nostrils of the Elders.

Yes, he admitted, that was the stuff, and he began to tell them how he had made it.

They scoffed. What, that well water! They drank.

Two of them revealed a rivalry which had hardly been suspected before, even by themselves. They fought. A man with a grey beard regarded a far horizon with eyes in which the light of an infinite understanding and kindliness shone. 'Stop them fighting,' he said, 'I want to talk.' But there was a man there who, though a bard, happened also to be trustworthy, and he started singing.

Meantime the Discoverer had at last helped himself, and presently the dull ache in his head was dispelled and a prompting to dance was balanced by a divine quiescence. Carefully he carried what was left of the liquor over beside the old man. 'Would you like another little drop?' he asked. 'Well, if you make it a small one,' replied the old man, who nevertheless was so taken with this magic drink that he helped himself to a stout measure. 'Canny!' shouted the Bard at him, interrupting his song to do so. And the fighters, catching the anxiety in the Bard's voice, called each other fools in strong language and joined the Bard.

As the sun went down they swore an immortal fellowship. The two fighters pricked their little fingers and ritually sealed a blood-brotherhood. But as for the rest of the world, not a word! Hush!

The atmosphere they carried about with them, however, was thick enough to stop a poisoned arrow. And at the very next distilling, the Elders surprised them.

So this was what all the mysterious silences and looks and enigmatic boastings—and smell—had been about! This was the unholy brew!

And just here—for all this may not be entirely irrelevant—it should be made clear that this folk were founded on what they called the democratic principle; that is to say, they believed that power ultimately resided in themselves, but for the smooth working of their community in peace and war, they found it convenient to elect Elders, a religious teacher or Druid, and a leader or Chief. It will thus be seen that they were a very primitive people; indeed so primitive that they were even prepared to fight for this democratic principle of theirs. And if that may seem obscure to many good Europeans now, still an effort should be made to understand it, were it only for this odd reason, namely, that it has persisted with an astonishing force among the elements of that folk to

9

this day. In seeking the reason for so strange a survival, even we may find ourselves compelled to dip into the well of the water of life.

During which time the Elders had drunk.

The others, including the Discoverer, watched and waited. No one had ever seen an Elder dance. Their eyes glistened unholily.

But the eyes of the Elders batted no eyelid. True, as the life-water had gone round, each had emitted a curious lengthy sound like a half-strangled cough. In after times this sound became well known, but then it was still young and charged with humorous surprise. To offset this expression, however, the Elders' faces immediately became unusually grave. Slowly each drew his hand down his beard, while his brows ridged in thought. They sat in a sun circle, which has neither precedence nor disruption, beginning nor end. As the life-water was making its third circuit, the Bard, who was prone to impatience, asked them for their finding.

They meditated in silence yet awhile, then the oldest Elder (they had the unbiological custom of respecting age) declared they had decided to take the matter to avizandum.

'What matter?' demanded the Bard.

'This matter,' responded the Elder, pointing to the second and last jarful. Whereupon he attempted to get up and after a little time succeeded. He looked very severe.

The other Elders concurred, with frowning glances at those around them.

'But you can't take that away!' shouted the Bard who, when not making poetry, was given to irreverence. 'I haven't had one yet!'

'You'll go without, then,' said the Elder.

'I'm damned if I will!'

'You'll be damned anyway,' said the Elder, whose eyes now had a piercing and terrible power. 'And moreover, if you speak again I'll report you to the Druid and have you up before the Session.' The vehemence in so old a man was astonishing.

'Report away!' shouted the Bard in a right fury.

The Elders began moving away with the evidence. The Bard swung round upon the others to incite them, but the Discoverer, catching his eye, winked slowly, and presently said to him in a low voice, 'I smuggled a jar round the corner.'

Looking after the Elders and noting their solemn if uncertain gait, the Bard broke into loud laughter. In a little while his companions were all dissolved in this laughter.

'You weren't very civil to him, all the same. What'll you say if we're had up?'

But the Bard was now on the crest of creation and finished his improvisation with a roar:

'. . . *civil?*
With usquebea we'll face the devil! '

Druids and chiefs, clans and federated clans, became the sport of their thought, the playthings of their wit.

But on the Seventh Day, the Druid preached from the text, ' The water of life—*and of death*,' and divided his discourse under many heads. It was a cogent exhaustive piece of work, within the subtle pattern of which there began to glimmer an eldritch fire, a loch of fire growing big as a sea, convoluting and molten and tinct of brimstone. Certain of the listeners felt themselves fall in and sink—and sink—and sink . . . ' yet though you keep on sinking to all eternity you will never reach the bottom.'

On the way home, the Bard tried to persuade the Discoverer to go to the hill stream, but the Discoverer would not go with him.

' Frightened? ' said the Bard. ' Humph! But I wonder how he knew so much about it? '

' It's his business to think Hell out,' said the Discoverer simply.

' Hell? Who's talking of Hell? I mean, how did he know so much about uisgebeatha? *Who drank the Elders' jar?* '

The Discoverer stopped dead, and on his face appeared evidence of the eternal dichotomy in the spirit of his tribe : wonder and fear, reverence and unholiness, wild laughter in an awful hush, saint and demon. He would put in authority those whom he would take down. For he was branded by the One God with the awful brand of the undying individualist.

'It's all right,' said the Bard. 'They would never suspect us so soon after the sermon.' And as they went on their way he added thoughtfully, 'This is a new thing and we'll have to think it out for ourselves.'

And it seems he was right, for his tribe are still making the usquebeatha, and still thinking it out— nearly as violently as ever.

★   ★   ★

As a story, it should end there : yet it would not be quite complete if it did, and as this is rather a grave matter for all that it may seem light and fanciful to many, I must introduce the Chief to show how, despite all the divisions that arose between that people and their Elders and Druid, they were as one in the marrow of the bone.

The Chief had secret ambitions. He dreamed of Power. This was a common pastime of all leaders, of course, and amongst other tribes they were usually able to gratify their wishes and consolidate their position in a feudal or other tyranny. But it was not so in this tribe that worshipped the democratic principle.

A maddening principle to the Chief, gnawing his secret passion. How often he had thought of the folk that lived over the border, a willing compromising people! In his bones he felt he could impose on them his ultimate dream of the Divine Right of Chiefs. Here if he tried anything out of the way, they would have the law on him as soon as look at him. There he might very easily make the one and final law: the Chief can do no wrong.

Now when this heady aspiration came in contact with the uisgebeatha, a transformation took place in the Chief's visage; as likewise in his whole body, which began to move with grace and assurance. And he was every inch a chiefly figure. The women admired him, and maids would play at putting white roses in their hair. But the Elders declared against interference with their neighbours. Their uncompromising manner so wrought upon him in anger that at last he cried out:

'Shut up! or I will clap a handful of Bishops on you!'

A tense, an awful, an enlightening silence ensued, through which came the Bard's voice: 'We prefer the Elders!'

' You what? '

' We prefer the Elders—such as they are.'

In this peculiar humour the Chief was momentarily lost, but he felt its sardonic power. He would never overcome this people. They would die, uncouth and damned, sooner; damned certainly. And by a sudden clairvoyance he saw that the uisgebeatha would help them. His dream of divine right was being filched away, smuggled away. . . .

' Who amongst you is the Smuggler? ' he shouted.

A man near the Bard was about to speak, but the Bard, knowing this man, stabbed him in the diaphragm with his elbow.

The Chief walked away alone.

The Bard turned towards the oldest Elder and said respectfully, ' What about——? ' lifting his eyebrows at the same time in the direction of the hill stream.

' I don't mind if I do,' answered the Elder. ' We have much to talk about.' There was a fine fire in his eyes, an unyielding fanaticism, and a grave smile.

EARLY HISTORY

I AM only too well aware that already the reader may consider I have laid too much stress on *uisgebeatha* as an original designation, as the very first 'water of life,' conveniently forgetting *aqua vitae* and *eau-de-vie*, or as Mr Aeneas Macdonald in his small but excellent book on this subject of *Whisky* says: 'There is a school which insists that *aqua vitae* is a corruption of *acquae vite*, "water of the wine." If this is indeed so, then it seems probable that in the earlier writers *aqua vitae* denotes a kind of brandy. But, on the other hand, the word "whisky" is derived from the Gaelic "*uisgebeatha*," which is "the water of life," a direct translation of the Latin *aqua vitae*.' Other modern writers have expressed the same idea.

Now I know that in this matter of whisky's antiquity (as so often of its age), there is confusion and uncertainty. We have, characteristically, no label bearing the whole truth. But, though no research scholar, I have hunted where I could, and with proper impartiality and, on so gracious a subject, with every desire to be courteous to the stranger,

I am yet compelled to the conclusion that *uisgebeatha* is not a direct translation from the Latin *aqua vitae*, but that *aqua vitae* is a direct translation from the Gaelic *uisgebeatha*.

Not that I am disposed to quarrel over it! But I should like to suggest that the time is at last approaching when we may with reasonable manners hint, or even smilingly affirm, that we were not necessarily savage because we were not Roman. The Celtic peoples had a civilization and were a great European power long before the Romans freed Barabbas. The historian Ephoros, in the fourth century B.C.,' substituted the Celts for the Ligurians among the three great peoples on the circumference of the world, and assigned to them the whole north-west of Europe as far as the borders of the Scythians ' (Hubert's *Rise of the Celts*). They attained the height of their power, in fact, at the same time as did the Latins. One of their maxims is recorded by a Greek: 'To worship the gods, to do nothing base, and to practise manhood.'

But there is another of their sayings, made direct to a Greek (or rather a Macedonian), that remains more readily in my mind. Taking all the circumstances into account, I think it about the profoundest retort in history. The occasion is that of Alexander the Great receiving Celts who had come 'for the purpose of making a treaty of friendship and mutual hospitality' (Strabo). Alexander was friendly, and whilst they were drinking together, asked them what they feared most in the world, 'supposing they would say it was he.' But the Celts replied, 'it was no man, only they felt some alarm lest the heavens should on some occasion or other fall on them.'

The manner of delivery must have been one of considerable suavity, for Alexander remained friendly, if astonished.

Emperors or Chiefs may not need quick wits or inspiration. Power in the grand sense is probably more potent than a whole hogshead of uisgebeatha. But the ambassadors, like some of our modern states-men, may well have taken a stimulant before going to so important a conference! Some of our greatest Scottish divines knew that conviction, zeal, inspiration, were warmed to the highest purpose by a small drop of whisky. For their arduous Sabbath duties and exhortations—beside which in cogency of reasoning and in spiritual depths the efforts of our modern pulpit men are little more than childish stammerings—their poor bodily frames had to be kept from drooping —and were so kept.

But try to imagine a great ambassador, a great statesman, or a great Scottish divine endeavouring to quicken his soul with beer or vintage port or chianti—admirable drinks in their time and place but never devised to whet the spirit sword-keen, to make it flash like Excalibur, or to give the assurance and bearing of a great protagonist.

Some of our finest modern political orators have found aid in champagne or brandy. But though champagne has liveliness it has not the ruthlessness of life; and brandy, for all its Ciceronian power, has in it the acknowledgment, the Roman dignity, of death. Already within it is the shadow of dissolution.

This matter, then, of the antiquity of uisgebeatha should be considered with no undue prejudice against the Celtic people. The prejudice is an old affair. Mr Aeneas Macdonald speculates with some reason that Dionysos was the god of whisky before he was the god of wine. He quotes the epigram made when Julian the Apostate, in his wars against ' the northern barbarians,' first encountered and disliked the barley brew. Let us extract the taunt:

' For lack of grapes from ears of grain your country-man, the Celt, made you.'

But I should like to know exactly why Julian grew so sarcastic. We do not loose our best shafts unless we are moved. Unfortunately it is not recorded what the barbarians thought of Julian and his sweetish grape-juice.

Our great difficulty indeed with these old Celts is

their aversion to writing of any kind. They believed in learning by heart. The Druidic schools were severe in their standards and austere in their methods. Certain it is, anyway, that at a very remote age the Celts acknowledged a potent god in the barley.

But our real concern here is the problem of distillation. Uisgebeatha or whisky is distilled from fermented barley water. Distillation may be defined as an operation that converts a substance into vapour and then condenses that vapour into liquid form. It is essentially very simple but very important. When you hold a cold plate to the steam from a kettle, the drops that form on the plate and run together make distilled water. Now no distilling process is gone through in making beer or wine. There are brewing and fermenting processes, but never does any of the liquor get boiled off and condensed back into liquid.

It is simple enough to distil any liquid, including wine. But when you distil wine, the result is brandy or *eau de vie*.

Thus it may be seen that in looking for the beginning of uisgebeatha we are also looking for a knowledge of distillation.

Did Julian drink brandy? We may certainly answer No. If the old Greeks and Romans were distillers of *aqua vitae* we should have heard about it. Aristotle does mention that pure water is made by the evaporation of sea water, and Pliny describes a primitive method of distillation, but there was obviously no accepted process or art of distilling amongst them.

But these two peoples did not make up the whole of the ancient world nor comprise all its knowledge. Hundreds of years before Julian, folk were manufacturing spirits (arrack) in India. The Chinese were expert distillers in remote times.

To the primitive form of still the Alexandrians gave a proper head, and the Arabians improved the cooling process by running cold water about a pipe that came away from the head—exactly as we do to-day.

How the early Celts went about it, of course we do not know, though if they devoted anything like the terrible concentration one of their young bards had to devote to learning his thousands of lines, I should not be in any way surprised to hear from some Eastern scholar that a certain adventuring Arabian brought home with him once upon a time from the fastnesses of the northern barbarians a still-head complete with worm (condensing pipe).

The earliest known reference to the preparation of spirits by distillation in Great Britain is contained in the Mead Song by the Welsh bard Taliessin in the sixth century :

' Mead distilled sparkling, its praise is everywhere.'

21

Obviously the clear distillate had a wide clientele.

Taliessin also has a Song to Ale, which shows his expert knowledge of the various stages in making a sound brew:

> ' He shall steep it in the Llyn
> Until it shall sprout.
> He shall steep it another time
> Until it is sodden.
> Not for a long time will be finished
> What the elements produce.
> Let his vessels be washed,
> Let his wort be clear.'

Under the headings of *Malting* and *Brewing* in the third part of this book, I have done little more than amplify these lines. And, in particular, how admirable are the last two!

The poem continues:

> ' And when there shall be an exciter of song,
> Let it be brought from the cell,'

(to prove to us that the Celts of that early century knew the value of a cellar!),

> ' Let it be brought before kings.
> In splendid festivals.
> Will not oppose every two
> The honey that made it.'

These last two lines are obscure, as are indeed many in old Taliessin. And Skene, from whose *The Four*

Ancient Books of Wales I have taken them, admits and honours the fact. But manifestly the word honey has some associative value in connection with the 'mead distilled sparkling.' Perhaps 'modern' poetry is not so modern as we suppose nor the prose of James Joyce altogether novel in its allusiveness.

This does go a little way, anyhow, towards confirming my suspicion that the Celtic bard was pretty early on the scene. The bardic tradition, like all those of ancient standing, was inclined to be academic and not at all given to innovation. Unless the Mead Song were a long-honoured theme, it would be as difficult for Taliessin to have it inscribed on the tablets of memory as it would be, say, for a young Oxonian to win the Newdigate with an effort on Hooch to a jazz rhythm.

Verses, of course, have been attributed to Taliessin that authorities quarrel over, and amongst them the well-known lines that foretold the coming of the Saxon into the land, his oppression of the Cymry, and his passing away when the day of his destiny should come. Probably there has just been enough of the prophecy fulfilled to make ardent Welshmen wonder!

> 'Their God they will praise,
> Their speech they will keep,
> Their land they will lose,
> Except wild Wales.'

At least this may be said, that if Taliessin's palate was as reliable as his prophetic gift, his praising of distilled mead must command our rspect.

These ancient Celts, then, were ' distillers,' ' kiln-distillers,' ' furnace-distillers.' So much seems certain.

*   *   *

When we get down to the intimate detail of distilling whisky, however, we come upon a matter of delicate difficulty.

All authorities agree that whisky or uisgebeatha, as we know it to-day, came originally from Scotland and Ireland, but whether from Scotland first or Ireland first, no one can definitely say. The important fact of origin having been established, however, I hardly think the question of precedence is of real concern. In any case, the link between Scotland and Ireland in ancient days was so close that in matters of vital interest there must have been pretty well spontaneous generation. The glens of Antrim and Tara Hall knew the gossip of Argyll before either Kerry or Caithness. Scholar's Gaelic—like our King's English—was common to both countries. And if Ireland comes into the picture first, it is because she was conquered first. (That last sentence may have an ambiguous ring to those who say that Scotland never was conquered. And, truly enough, Scotland never was conquered by force of arms. But it is hardly worth my while altering the sentence for all that.)

Happily for us, we know that distillation from fermented grain liquor was practised in Ireland *before* the distillation of wine was introduced. In other words, uisgebeatha preceded *eau-de-vie* so far as that country was concerned. There is an old Irish legend which credits St. Patrick with having first taught the Irish the art of distillation. From the many mysteries and marvels attributed by the Irish to St. Patrick, whom they made their patron saint, it is clear that he must have appeared to them as a man not only of high spiritual quality but of great knowledge and learning, a sort of superman, or visitor from ' another world.' He was born near Dumbarton on the Clyde.

But whether we credit the old Irish legend or not, certain it is that at the time of the first English invasion of Ireland (1170–72), the Irish were manufacturing a spirit distilled from grain.

The English brought back the art with them—or brought back the Irish who knew the art—and by the end of the century a home-produced spirit could be got at their apothecaries or vintners. The dissolution of the monasteries under Henry VIII resulted in many of the monks setting up in business as distillers, brewers, and vinegar makers.

The attachment of the Church to the interests of the distiller is notable throughout our history. At a comparatively recent date, a Scottish pulpit has been found a convenient place in which to conceal liquor from the prying eyes of the law. I remember how my school-books insisted that the monasteries were the centres of learning and culture and asylums for those fleeing from the secular arm. There was one near Inverness called Beau Lieu (now Beauly) which had appropriately advanced the fruitfulness of the soil to an extraordinary degree. Its pears, apples, and grain were famous. For reasons which I hope subsequently to make clear, I can have no great faith in the quality of the English liquor, but if there was a small still in operation in Beauly (in recent times the centre of a renowned smuggling area), I would give much to taste the liquor the apple-ripe monks distilled from the barley. In my time I have cast anxious eyes over the ruins of the ancient Priory, but at last and reluctantly I have given up all hope of coming on hidden treasure in a sealed jar.

As for *eau-de-vie*, the production of a spirit from wine does appear to have been known some three centuries *after* Taliessin sang in Wales; and one important authority asserts that the first effort at distilling wine in France took place in the thirteenth century. Altogether then, distilling of the barley brew by the Celtic people seems to have preceded by untold centuries distilling of fermented wine by Greek or Latin. In this matter of relative antiquity, uisgebeatha gets my vote. We knew the 'water of life' in the beginning.

LATER HISTORY

ALTHOUGH whisky was thus early distilled in Ireland and Scotland, it has had right through the centuries until a mere two to three hundred years ago what might be called a very poor press. Ossian appears to ignore it. The Fingalians, we gather, drank deep of ale or mead, thereby immediately putting us up against this difficulty: what sort of ale and what sort of mead? Was the ale the famous Heather Ale, concerning which Neil Munro tells so well the legendary story? If so, it was brewed out of more than heather-tops, for though the bees suck there to make their finest honey, no purplest bloom offers in sufficient degree the necessary basis of alcohol. At any rate, such a mildly fermented drink as would have been concocted would certainly be classed to-day for revenue purposes as non-alcoholic. Heather ale was not so simple as all that if the Picts had a hand in it! And we do know that in some of the Western Isles a very potable liquor was still being brewed from two parts heather-tops to one part malt in the eighteenth century. From the malt is got the *saccharine basis* without which alcohol cannot be obtained. It is important to remember that. Honey or mead has got that saccharine basis and alcohol could have been distilled from it.

That this word alcohol, by the way, as we now use it, is of comparatively recent date may be as surprising to many as that the first references to the word whisky are to be found no earlier than the beginning of the eighteenth century. The Oxford Dictionary gives an Arabic origin for alcohol: ' from the particle *al* and the word *kohl*, an impalpable powder used in the East for painting the eyebrows.' What connection there may be between painted eyebrows and alcohol as we know it, I have been quite unable to discover.

Regarding the matter judicially, then, I am not finally satisfied that one of these terrible Fingalian heroes faded away on a honey brew or even that a Viking went berserk on ale. Centuries after this, historians may be troubled at so ardent a people as the Americans ' going blind ' on a drink with the homely name of rye. Burns referred to whisky as ' barley bree.' In other words, at the back of much of this talk of Gael and Teuton in Scotland, there is not only verbal ambiguity but, far more importantly, that dark fellow the Pict. He was engaged on Christian missionary work of the highest kind a

hundred and fifty years before Columba, the statesman, fled from Ireland to Iona, taking, alas, his
statesmanship with him. The Pict may possibly have
had a lot to answer for very early. Clearly he had
the brains to work potent marvels, and certainly
produced a Monster in Loch Ness to frighten Columba,
as Adamnan relates at length. (Contrast Inverness
Town Councillors of to-day who, when the Monster
appears, are as astonished as any foreigner. Does
not even so simple a matter reflect how steep the
decline in native knowledge and power?)

But of all the marvels related by the wise and
learned Adamnan, who himself ruled in Iona as one
of the successors to Columba, that which impressed
me most was his reference to the Picts having *drinking
glasses.*

*   *   *

From which reflections a monstrous thought up-
rears its head. How did it happen that the Picts
passed away, like Shakespeare's cloud-capped towers
and solemn temples, leaving not a rack behind?
As the Maglemosians vanished before them? And
as the Gael is ebbing away after them with the utter
inevitability of an uncorked bottle? Can it be—
horror!—that the white logic of the water of life
reflects the face of civilization as the face of an idiot-

Narcissus? That the whole game is not worth putting
the cork back for? Have I stumbled here by chance
on what whisky has really meant to Scotland? It is
a profound thought, and one to which I hope solemnly
to return. I am aware of a certain strange excitement
' enwrought with light.' It may be possible to learn
what the Discoverer felt, silent by his little hill stream.

*　　　*　　　*

Let me pass quickly, therefore, over such historical
references as that James IV, perhaps our ablest and
surely our most versatile King, had his *aqua vitae*
made from barley by a friar, the transaction being
recorded in the Exchequer Roll if not by a Court
poet of the period. In truth, the fact seems to be
that uisgebeatha was not recognized by a proper gentleman as a courtly drink. It was—in a curiously strict
sense—a distillate of the people. No one really sang
it until Burns appeared. The true importance of
this may be seen later when we come to discuss that
' monstrous thought.'

Round about 1600 the whisky business began to
hum. There was much traffic between Highlands
and Lowlands, and in the Outer Isles the chiefs agreed
(1609) to the ' Statutes of Icolmkill.' From these
statutes it would appear that the poverty of the Isles
and the ' cruelty and inhuman barbarity ' of their

feuds were due to an inordinate love of 'strong wines and aqua-vitae.' Accordingly power was given to any person to seize without payment wine or 'aqua-vitae' imported for sale; and anyone who bought such liquor from a mainlander incurred severe penalties. The Isles were thus made what we might call a closed area. Yet—and this is the important point— it was declared lawful for an individual to brew as much aqua-vitae as his own family might require. (The 'barons and wealthy gentlemen' were, of course, permitted to purchase on the mainland what-ever wine or other liquor they needed.) There can be no question but that the aqua-vitae mentioned is whisky. The islanders had no grapes to make *eau-de-vie-de-vin*. And so we are posed with such interest-ing questions as: Was it the custom for each family to have its own still? Did the consumption of whisky *not* breed poverty and inhuman barbarity? How and to what extent did the Islesman drink his whisky?

Of the last question, I will say this: I knew of Highland families in which whisky was as naturally in the home as milk. It was consumed as a normal Englishman will consume a glass of beer—when he needs it, with food (a dram *before* food, for the Gael. Our fashionable cocktail had at least a decent ancestor), or for convivial occasion. Even lads of school age would get a drop of whisky when they physically needed it. And I have never known in my own experience—nor learned from another—of any such lad ever becoming in after life a drunkard. To abuse so natural a gift of the life-giving barley would have been looked upon as a weakness akin to some curious form of moral decrepitude. But such drinks as wines and brandies, they were new and exciting as would have been ladies with painted eyebrows; they were disturbances from beyond the home, they stood for the romantic outside world, for licence and debauch.

It is only from some such angle that these liquor restrictions in the Statutes of Icolmkill become half-logical or reasonable to me.

Again, in 1616, the Privy Council passed an ' Act agens the drinking of Wynes in the Yllis,' referring to ' beastly and barbarous cruelties and inhumanities ' from this wine drinking, and ordaining that none of the ' tenants and commons ' of the Isles shall at any time ' heirefter buy or drink ony wynes in the Yllis or continent nixt adiacent under the pane of twenty pounds '—one-half of the said pane to go to the King's Majesty and the other half to their ' masters and landlords and chieftains ' for their private use.

In 1622 another Act was passed prohibiting merchants and skippers from sending or carrying wines to the Isles under the pain this time of complete confiscation of the cargo—'except so meikle as is allowed to the chieftains and gentlemen of the Ilis.' In this Act we get the picture: 'When there arrives any ship or other vessel there with wines they spend both days and nights in their excess of drinking and seldom do they leave their drinking so long as there is any of the wine left' and so 'there falls out many inconveniences amongst them to the break of His Majesty's peace.' My only regret is that the Gaelic poets of that time and place, being poets of the people, had not their view of the matter fixed in writing. But, like Ossian and Homer, they neither read nor wrote; and as for their poor brethren they learned by heart instead of by eye, and so would have roared out epic or satire over the gushing scarlet of Bordeaux like the barbarians they were!

Poverty, cruelty, inhuman barbarity. It is as devastating a charge as could be levelled against any cannibal islanders, and being contained in an actual legal enactment, must surely be beyond any possibility of explaining away?

Let us go back for a moment to these 'Statutes of Icolmkill' to which the chiefs themselves put their hands. The sixth Statute deals with education. In its preamble the 'continuance of barbarity, impiety and incivility' within the Isles is attributed to the neglect of education, as the children were not sent to the mainland to be trained in virtue, learning, and the English tongue. It was laid down that every 'gentil-man or yeaman' within the said Islands . . . shall put at the least their eldest son or having no children male, their eldest daughter to the schools in the lowland . . . . there to bring them up until they 'may be found sufficiently to speik, reid, and write Inglische.' In short, their real concern in all this was that the 'Irishe language which is one of the chief and prin-cipall causis of the continewance of barbaritie and incivilitie amongis the inhabitants of the Isles and Heylandis may be abolisheit and removeit.'

King James VI of Scotland, now become King James I of England, together with his advisers had set out on a project that aimed at nothing less than the extinction of the Gaelic tongue.

The barbarity was the barbarity of a classic language, the cruelty is unspecified, and the poverty—could afford to buy shiploads of wine and hold high carnival for 'both days and nights.'

As for their own uisgebeatha not being so strong as wine, that is of course quite absurd, even if Martin, in his *Description of the Western Isles of Scotland* (*circa* 1695), did not explain that 'their plenty of corn was such, as disposed the natives to brew several sorts of liquor, as common usquebaugh, another called trestarig, *id est*, aqua-vitae, three times distilled, which is strong

35

and hot; a third sort is four times distilled, and this by the natives is called usquebaugh-baul, *id est* usquebaugh, which at first taste affects all the members of the body: two spoonfuls of this last liquor is a sufficient dose; and if any man exceed this, it would presently stop his breath, and endanger his life.'

As for the customs and social life of the people of the Isles, Martin's precise description of them seemed yet so extraordinary that no less a personage than the London-loving Dr Johnson set out on a voyage of discovery. Not that Johnson could gather much, for all the marvellous wealth of Gaelic poetry and story and folk-song was hidden from him.

But what I am concerned with here is not the rebuttal of legal misrepresentation: it is the subtle method of discrediting and destroying the way of life of a people, and I should like the reader to remember it when we presently give the subject its head.

Meantime it explains by implication not only the smuggling that was carried on in the Highlands to such an extent in comparatively recent times because of the duty (regarded by the people—who had always, as we have seen, made their own uisgebeatha at home— as unnatural a violation of God's providence as the Game Laws), but also the ungodly charges that were levelled against the smugglers. Perhaps, also, a man's character is not ennobled by being hunted, and where he has to drink by stealth he too often drinks to excess, as respectable Scotland knows!

*   *   *

It would be impossible, even were it necessary, to trace here the interesting company in which whisky found itself right on through the Covenanting period to the last Jacobite rising. Prince Charlie himself had his short desperate adventure with whisky before he relapsed into the death of brandy. (Perhaps there is a profounder symbolism here than may readily appear.) Hanoverian agents did their best to get Highlanders to betray their fellows by 'filling them drunk with whisky' in accordance with the recognized principles of political espionage if not with success. But we hope to be concerned with something more important, more fatally significant, than the romantic minutiæ of our subject before we are done. In the main, as Burns makes clear in his *Scotch Drink*, whisky was 'the poor man's wine,' compared with which brandy was but 'burning trash.'

If that is now understood, then perhaps we may refer to the Jacobite army's commissariat being well supplied with whisky without anticipating cruelties and inhuman barbarities. Actually the whole march to Derby was carried through with such absence of atrocity as places it in this respect pretty nearly without parallel in history. Mr Evan M. Barron, in his admirable preface to the second edition of his *Scottish War of Independence*, quotes from the hostile author of the Woodhouselee MS. : 'never did 6000 thieving ruffians with uncouth weapons make so harmless a march in a civilized plentiful country.' As for the Covenanting times, we have what has been called with ruck of slighting adjectives, the 'Highland Host.' The drunken self-seekers in Edinburgh—Scots like Lauderdale, under power from London, what infamous dogs they have so often been!—planted 6000 Highlanders, along with some Lowland militia, in Ayrshire ostensibly to suppress the Covenanters, but actually to provoke insurrection, so that estates might be forfeited—for the good of the friends of the Commissioners! Each Highlander of the Host, we gather, had as great a concern for the flask of whisky as for his claymore.

> 'There's yet I have forgotten
> Which ye prefer to roast or sodden,
> Wine and wastle, I dare say,
> And that is routh of usequebay.'

Amid a scene of intense religious excitement, with all the deeper feelings of man inflamed, with house-searching, persecution, and spoliation the order of the day, the Highland Host were well set for the bloodiest ongoings. In fact, the commission granted

to the leaders of the Host exonerated them before-
hand from all blame ' no matter what excesses their
followers might commit.' Actually the Highlanders
withdrew, after having been quartered on the ' rebels '
from January to March (1678), without having caused
a single death: a more remarkable feat than that
performed by the Jacobite army!

This is not an effort at praising the Scots, whether
in the Isles or in Ayrshire. When driven on it, they
can be more remorselessly annihilating than most.
They have a record in Empire wars that should last
them until—however it will help them at—the
Judgment Day. All I am trying to suggest is that
the Scot, before he was badgered and pestered by
political intrigue and oppression, could treat his
whisky as a Frenchman has never had to forget how
to treat his wine.

It was the lords and gentlemen who set the fashion
of drunkenness in that eighteenth century of claret
and brandy and rum. Burns, in *The Whistle*, com-
memorates a gargantuan contest between three lairds.
When a seventh bottle of claret disappears down his
friend's throat in one bumper, the ' cautious and
sage ' Glenriddle, with six empty bottles behind him,
gets to his feet:

> ' A high-ruling elder to wallow in wine!
> He left the foul business to folks less divine.'

Claret is a kingly wine, and brandy and rum can have, I believe, an insidious attraction. But from the wholesale character of their consumption by the 'upper classes' of Scotland (a proper host was offended with a guest who had not to be carried to bed), I am not sure that there was a great deal of concern for those qualities that distinguish good liquor from indifferent. The whisky that Burns drank must have been fairly rough stuff, yet it manifestly had palatable qualities superior to 'burning trash.' And Burns knew about brandy. He was a guest at the contest for the Whistle, and is believed to have drunk during the course of the evening a bottle of brandy and a bottle of rum.

The real fact of the matter seems to be that whisky was still regarded as common and claret and brandy as fashionable.

Times or fashions have changed in a manner that is apt to make us look back on that intercourse with the wines of Bordeaux as pleasant and civilized, perpetuating in its way an earlier and more real intercourse with the customs and scholarship of the Continent.

(Had I to contrast, in passing, the respective merits and after-effects of drunkenness by whisky and by claret, all I should be prepared to say is that those upper classes would have had my profound sympathy.)

40

A duty was imposed on whisky in 1660, but claret was still being allowed into the country free in 1780. This is not specially mentioned as another injustice to Scotland! Heavily fortified wine—far more potent than the claret of those days—is being allowed into this country at the present moment at a duty of less than one-seventh the whisky rate. It is the sort of thing that normally happens to Scotland—by accident, of course, for as we know the fates are blind (if, occasionally, surely blind drunk).

From being a drink made in a man's home, whisky now became an affair of public manufacture. Forbes of Culloden (the man who broke the rising of 1745) held the estate of Ferintosh, whereon he had the famous Brewery of Aquavity. In 1689 it was raided by ' Highland rebels ' with whom Forbes was not in favour; whereupon the Government passed a special Act of Parliament (it had time in those days to attend to such homely affairs), farming out to him and his successors the yearly Excise of the lands of Ferintosh for about £22. Presently more whisky was being distilled at Ferintosh than in all the dutiable rest of Scotland together, and Forbes's annual profit was reckoned out at about £18,000. There were jealous complaints, and when in 1707 the Board of Excise was established, representations were made frequently to the Treasury. But not until 1784 was the owner bought out for the sum of £21,000. Burns's lament has often been quoted:

> ' Thou Ferintosh, O sadly lost!
> Scotland laments frae coast to coast!
> Now colic grips and barking hoast
>   May kill us a',
> For loyal Forbes' chartered boast
>   Is ta'en awa'.'

During that golden century for the real victors of Culloden the duty had risen from threepence to about four shillings a gallon. We have entered upon whisky's modern phase. Questions of duty and the evasions, adulterations, and horrible substitutes to which they gave birth, we may briefly consider in a later part of this book. Meantime it is enough to learn that in the year 1823 there were 14,000 official detections of illicit distillation. In succeeding years before an ever-increasing revenue vigilance, they steadily declined, until in 1874 only six detections were recorded. (In 1934 there were seven detections.) But in that year of 1874 a great number of illicit stills must actually have been at work. Old men all over the north and west of Scotland have told me smuggling stories of their early boyhood that would fill a few volumes. The other day I was handling the actual glass balls used by a certain Banffshire smuggler for testing the strength of the liquor. My friend, who now possesses them, has not yet quite reached the allotted span, but he remembers very vividly how his elders would gather now and then and make a joyous evening with fun and story and Boshen's whisky. Boshen was a crofter, and the farmers and crofters in his neighbourhood sent him barley and received back whisky, just as they sent oats to the mill and received back meal. There was no real sense of guilt in this transaction, any more than in taking a salmon by stealth from the river. If the sensitive were troubled at all, it was by the guilt of evasion, not of moral wrong. Mostly they were decent God-fearing men and women, who would have been shocked and grief-stricken at any son who would have stolen a penny.

This may be difficult to grasp by one who does not understand the background from which such thought and action naturally emerged. To the poor Scot, deriving from the ancient Gaelic social life, ideas in property and ownership of certain fruits of earth and sea were radically different from those of a poor Anglo-Saxon deriving from feudalism: so much so that it was a difference not merely in conscious idea but in blood impulse. I should like to stress this, because unless it is grasped I may go on talking about Scotland and what whisky has meant to her to the crack of doom and yet convey nothing but a fury of superficial and (no cause being seen) irrelevant happenings.

And so we swing back again to our starting point with the Celts as the makers of whisky. Fundamentally we are concerned with the commons of Scotland, whether in the Yllis of the Statutes or the Ayrshire of Burns. They and their whisky are one.

For a time, accordingly, we shall appear to leave whisky directly, in order to follow after that monstrous thought which reared its head a little while ago! Before we can know what whisky has meant to Scotland, presumably we must first have some idea of what Scotland means to herself. This may take us on a flying excursion from self-expression to nationalism, but I promise to devote the third part of this book to whisky's own self.

PART II
THE SPIRIT

THE FATED CELTS

I KNOW that to many minds I have been indulging
in a piece of special pleading for the Celt, or his
more homely representative, the Gael. Perhaps I
have. But what I should really like to understand
is why this should rouse a curious sort of instinctive
hostility. Is not the reader conscious of a very slight
(or not so slight) impatience at the mere idea of
having to discuss ' this Gaelic civilization business ' ?
From my experience—and at the moment I believe
I am perfectly, even pleasantly, detached—the reader
is. And his answer to Why ? might take the normal
form of : ' I'm fed up with all this Gaelic and haggis
and tartan and whisky business ! What have they
ever done anyway ? ' And lest any English reader
should think I am referring exclusively to him, let
me say at once that the reaction indicated is not only
more common in certain Scots but far stronger and
at times whole-heartedly virulent.

Yet manifestly the answer is a psychological ' blind.'
Gaelic is dying steadily, there is more haggis consumed
in London on one particular night of the year than

in Caledonia in probably a whole year, the tartan is worn not by the native working Highlander but by the shooting tenant or his kind, the majority of whom are not Scots, and whisky is so dear that a working man can afford little more than a smell of the cork. And as for what these things have ever done, they are certainly doing one thing now with efficient despatch and that is dying.

Again, if the reason for the impatience or irritability were genuine, why should the guying of these things on the stage by Scotch comedians provoke such immoderate mirth? Study the audience and you will observe the pleasure is rich to the point of being nearly voluptuous.

I admit this is beginning to look like a case for psychoanalysis! Any member of that audience (excluding teetotallers) would, for example, find nothing but genuine pleasure in listening to G. K. Chesterton praising up English pubs and English beer, or describing in panegyric the English countryside or any of the ancient customs and habits of the Anglo-Saxon, or reading a poem in praise of grocers, or doing all he could to hold to what was simple and medieval and to damn what was mechanistic and modern. Not all would agree with him, but all would understand and enjoy him. And even those who disagreed would be left with a certain nostalgia, including even the brightest of young things, who indeed love to indulge the week-end habit of dashing off to little country inns, complete with simple life and all that.

Or, again, how pleasant to follow a tour of the vineyards of France, to string the lovely names, to sit in the village cafés, to gather the local lore, to visit the châteaux, to get at the ancient soul of that great land! No impatience here, no irritability, no desire to guy and laugh and destroy.

What I have tried to isolate may well appear an extraordinary manifestation of the modern spirit. But it is not modern only. Almost from the beginnings of recorded history, there has been a world drive against the Celts. This to me has long been at once the most remarkable and enigmatic of all the historic movements of the human species. I know of no one who has attempted to understand and explain it, though I was pleased to find that M. Hubert, probably the greatest modern savant on the Celtic peoples, explicitly stated the fact in his recently published and invaluable two volumes: *The Rise of the Celts* and *The Greatness and Decline of the Celts.* ' If we look carefully at the map we shall see that the districts where they are found are refuges. The Celts came to a stop there at the sea, clinging to the rocks. Beyond the sea was their next world. They stayed on the shore, waiting for the ferry, like the dead in Procopios.' And again : ' What now remains of the Celts, in the west of their ancient dominion, was driven there and confined there by other peoples arriving or growing up behind them. This general movement of expansion and contraction taking the Celts to the west and confining them there may be called the law of Celticism. It must be studied as a capital fact of European history.'

And the process is still going on, none the less deadly or ruthless because in these days it may be less bloody—the process of driving them off the ultimate rocks into the sea. In this sense the Scotch comedian, well paid by the ' other peoples ' to make them laugh at his Celtic guying, is quite literally a capital fact in European history !

Put like that, it sounds rather amusing, but let us think it out. And it might help us, give us a better perspective, if we switched over from our own island to Ireland, where the Celt is most alive and assertive.

Now I suggest that there exists generally in Britain a deep-rooted feeling against Ireland. The nature of this feeling is very difficult to describe and, when surprised, it proves anything but rational. When thoroughly roused, it can evoke extraordinary deeps of bitterness. No mere matter of political differences explains it. It is far more profound than the transitory national hatreds roused by war. There is in it something quite virulent, like an instinctive urge to annihilate what one dislikes or hates or fears.

This may seem an excessive estimate. My experience assures me that it is restrained. I have found that I can always push the argument until I am told flatly that the only solution to the 'Irish problem' is to sink the whole damned island in the Atlantic. Sweet reasonableness only increases opposition. An English army man, a decent genial fellow, not at all given to hates, once assured me with superb tolerance: 'The individual Irishman is all right, but the Irish in the mass are bloody.'

If Ireland could be totally submerged for a few days then lifted up again and colonized by decent stock, would Britain—or would she not—heave a sigh of relief? I respectfully suggest that an attempt should be made to answer the question honestly—and, incidentally, to interpret 'decent.'

Or let us glance at Celtic Wales, where Taliessin sang. What do we think of the Welsh? When the argument is pursued in a public house, what comes back by way of encomium? 'Taffy was a Welshman, Taffy was a thief . . .' made a pleasant school jingle even in the far north of Scotland in my young days. We laughed at an ending to the rhyme that we would not have repeated within hearing of a drunken drover.

I am aware that all this looks as though I were suggesting that the Anglo-Saxon is the implacable enemy of the Celt and will never be happy until he has completely absorbed or submerged him. And do not let us confuse the issue here by saying that there are Celts in Cheshire and Lothian as there are Anglo-Saxons in Wales and Ireland, while there are mixtures everywhere. The ethnological debate is without end. Quite simply, Ireland and the Irish mean something very definite to England and the English. We know it and have acted upon it to the shedding of blood.

But, and this is my point, England is not the only country where the animus is found. After all, England has some normal reasons for a healthy dislike of the Celtic fringe. She has battled with it long enough, tried to subdue it with varying success over long and sanguinary periods. She may be forgiven a certain wariness and mistrust on historic counts.

But the animus, as I have indicated, may be found in Scotland often in a bitterer form than in England. It is also to be found in the Free State, and may be seen gaping from between the lines of the weekly summary by ' Our Irish Correspondent ' in the British press.

There is a movement on foot in the Highlands, as I write this, to cut off the Outer Isles from the mainland counties of which they are an administrative part, and have them subsidized (or pauperized) by, and governed direct from, Westminster; or as one publicist put it, ' to cast them adrift into the Atlantic.'

Nor is this animus, conscious or otherwise, confined to the British Isles. Take France, the ancient Gaul, where one might expect to find least trace of it. Last year the International P.E.N. Congress—a conference of writers—met in Scotland. When M. Crémieux, the distinguished French critic, had returned to France he wrote an impression of his visit for the *Modern Scot*, a quarterly devoted to literature. ' I shall not easily forget,' he wrote, ' the rush of the bourgeois Scottish intellectuals towards the bottles of sherry and whisky.' ' Tartans, kilts, reels, bagpipes, Gaelic, all this eternal local colour belongs more to a small country than to the genuine primitive. One cannot go on forever lamenting the woes of Mary Stuart.' And he concludes by asking if this is the time to be indulgent to nationalism.

From a Frenchman, by the way, this doubting of the wisdom of being indulgent to nationalism has a certain aptitude. Perhaps we have all been hocussed by the armament-controlled press, and actually the French and Germans are arranging to have themselves governed jointly from Geneva, and any day may spring this delightful surprise on wearied old Europe. On the surface, however, it merely appears that a Frenchman is not prepared to give up his nationalism but with his life—and the lives of half the rest of the world.

That may be forgiven him, but the sherry *and* whisky is another matter. We may be uncouth, but not to the verge of such ambiguity. Sherry *or* whisky, yes; the rush of the bourgeois intellectuals, possibly (compare the rush at Killiecrankie); but that any Scot going (not to mention rushing) for whisky might be deflected by sherry suggests a rather horrible indecency in M. Crémieux' fancy, were we not aware of his innocence.

And it is an interesting innocence; it is in fact part of the answer I put into the mouth of any Anglo-Scot in the opening paragraph of this section. M. Crémieux makes even a courteous effort to define his terms. The kilt, we observe, is a dress suitable for a small country. (The smaller the better?) That the bagpipes are not genuine primitive would be a very considerable advance upon English opinion, were it not that M. Crémieux considers the genuine primitive 'something from which we have declined.' But I think he hits the last nail on the head when he includes Gaelic in 'local colour.' It's a long cry to

Lochowe! shouted the Campbells, when raiding in Caithness. It's a longer cry from the early centuries of our era when Gaelic scholars set out to Christianize some barbarians in Europe, when the Gaelic tongue was already skilled in metrical devices and philosophy, and when its folk-lore or mythology was as fine as the Greeks', with morality added.

In all sorts of ways, by all sorts of peoples, then, that which is Celtic or Gaelic has been driven back to the mountains, driven into the sea. Until at last, among many of the Gaels themselves, a shame of their heritage comes over them, and they have been known to deny it with a curious and introverted hate.

Why this should be so, we really do not know. Perhaps the Celts have no world function to fulfil, or had so old a one that we have forgotten it. Or perhaps, as M. Hubert says, they were not conquerors, they were civilizers. They were the makers of whisky.

THE DESCENT

AND whisky faithfully accompanied them in our land, beneficent and genial when the way of life was their own way, and they feared only that the sky would fall on them; but drawing nearer to them as ' other peoples ' for their profit began to worry and hunt them.

The hunt went on, physical escape became more and more difficult, so whisky came still nearer, offering forgetfulness to the mind itself, until in the end when their misery had become too great, it plunged them in orgies of drunkenness the like of which the world can rarely have seen.

There may be something in the old notion of polarity—where there is love there is hate, where there is height there is depth. Let us hope so, for otherwise there would be no explaining the depth of unutterable squalor to which whisky accompanied the folk of Scotland in the industrial era. Whisky was the true witch's brew, the real bottled spirit of the Satanic master. No sink of iniquity but it made more loathsome; no wretchedness it could not make vile.

It reigned in the vennels and the wynds and the closes; it held court in the backlands; it crept on stealthy feet into the streets of the petty bourgeoisie turning clerks and storekeepers into sly chuckling simulacra of men. Here it began to lose hold of the women, who came to hate it with a hatred that never left them, an ineffable horror that holds sway in many of the quiet unobtrusive streets of our cities to this day. The young office-men of Glasgow, for example, are now coffee drinkers; and if one of them should take a whisky he does so by stealth. I know men of over thirty who resort to the usual methods to destroy the taint of whisky in their breaths lest their mothers smell it; not for any esoteric mother-complex reason, but because quite simply they remember boyhood days when they or their companions were sent out to hunt the public houses and the infamy that then often befel them as they attempted to lure drunken fathers to the women who waited.

That is what whisky essentially means to the vast body of respectable Scots. And the word respectable is used in no silly or superior manner. The reaction here is so instantaneous, so impulsive, that the very title of this book will evoke vistas of endless misery and shame *and nothing else*. It may be difficult for peoples of other countries to understand this, to appreciate the instinctive abhorrence, to envisage the loathing that turned away (as it so often had to turn away) from displayed vomit.

I know a dear old lady whose son was once so very ill that the doctor prescribed spirits to keep the heart going. (In solemn or respectable social moments, whisky was always called spirits. In this way what was repellent in the awful word itself was smoothed over a little. In similar manner, doctors or nurses at the bedside may refer to the natural functions.)

It was a moment of grave decision for the mother and with all the desperation and tragedy of it in her face, she looked at the doctor and said, ' I would sooner that he died.' But being the true Scots mother she did not let it rest there. She at once proceeded to get in touch with another doctor who, she knew, would in no circumstances prescribe spirits. And he came and he did not prescribe spirits. The son recovered and the triumph was thus not only over death but—over whisky. And it is the second part of the triumph that is beginning to develop the moving note of legend.

Now to describe this aspect of whisky—the only aspect to so many—would be first of all to describe in some detail the social condition of the people in the industrial areas of Scotland during the rise of the industrial era. For fundamentally what was to blame was the material or social condition of the people.

Children of five or six years of age working fourteen hours a day, thrashed into continuous wakefulness, and buried, like the slaughtered in battle, in a common field; colliers enslaved to their mines, malformed or deformed beasts of burden; slums within slums; filth only one shade less appalling than poverty; wretchedness and squalor from the narrow evil wynds of Dundee to the infected warrens of the Glasgow closes. It is a picture that can hardly be overdrawn, however sombre the mind or dark the colours.

But it is happily not my business to attempt the picture. All that concerns us here is that the folk, who had to have some sort of escape if they were to save themselves from being permanently debased, found that escape in whisky. Whisky took them out of themselves, it liberated them to blasphemy and fighting, it lifted their heads to shout a final challenge, a Yea hideous in the mouth but affirmative, it caressed them, and finally made of the gutter a bed of forgetfulness.

Whisky, as we have seen, was the drink of the people; the national drink. At this hideous period whisky became the national whore and lost her reputation so utterly that to this day even English Chancellors of the Exchequer continue to squeeze the last shilling of her immoral earnings out of her with an exorbitant shamelessness.

True, there is a considerable body of great poetry about the woman of joy, the scarlet woman; and the Founder of our religion let her anoint His feet. But understanding or insight or pathos of so final a kind is not expected here; yet it does occur to me to wonder why those who were (and still are) repelled abhorrently by whisky were not infinitely more repelled by the social conditions which let whisky act so revealingly. One would think that whisky had been the *cause* of the state of the poor, that it had built the slums and ensured the poverty, that it was the whole monstrous creator of that economic hell. In this attitude there is something so cowardly that it is difficult always to have complete patience with it. One may readily have patience with the women who, being realists, condemned the drunken horrors they saw. But with the so-called social and temperance reformers, as with the religious and political rulers, patience is less easy, for it is natural to expect that they would have made some effort to see through the effect to the cause, and, once having seen, to have become the people's impassioned leaders against the savagery of a system that produced such appalling results.

But not only did they support the social order (many seeing in it the righteous handiwork of a God who had called each to his appointed place), but were themselves of the owning or governing class who hunted and persecuted so brutally such ' friends of the people ' as, haunted by humanity's vision of liberty and fraternity, dared raise a voice in the people's favour. There is something in this so pusillanimous, so pharisaical, so (consciously or unconsciously) evil, that to me at least the mere alcoholic phase does little more in comparison than call for whatever Christian charity or pity may be found in a man's heart or stomach.

And so I propose to leave it at that, though I am aware that many will expect me to grub about in the alcoholic degradation in order to find all sorts of lessons and horrid warnings! In our story it is only a phase, however, and its worst excesses are lessening in precise correspondence with the improvement in the social order. Presently when our preoccupation with the larger racial theme brings us to consider the more immediate modern problems of nationalism and war, the economic argument may crop up again, and then discussing nationalism may be like discussing whisky—at one passionless remove!

Meantime all I am sure of is that so deep an impression did generations of drunkenness make on the Scottish scene that it will undoubtedly be visited upon any writer who sets out to compile a book in favour of whisky! He is asking for maledictions and will

receive them. In the hearts of countless decent folk
he will be regarded as a blasphemer and a monster.
Amongst those who ' tak' up their dram ' in modera-
tion, he will be considered a quite needless adventurer,
for even if a man does slip an occasional ' quick one '
down his throat that is no reason why the matter
should be given publicity. As for the hard secret
drinker, he will experience the fear of certain burrow-
ing forms of life for any sort of light. And even
amongst those who drink openly and in defiance of
kirk and banker, the uproarious rebels, the poets and
navvies and novelists, there will be hearty encourage-
ment to go full steam ahead, to give it to old Calvin
in the neck, to rock all canting hypocrisy to its rotten
feet, to have an orgy and sing the roof off the inhibited
camphor-smelling vacuum that is the respectable
Scottish mind. To very few indeed will it occur
that the subject should be treated naturally, with
quiet earnestness, with pleasure in its contemplation,
with whatever grace the writer may possess. How
far have we wandered from the ' water of life ' !

WHY?

THAT idea of having wandered far from our true heritage brings us back again to consideration of our Celtic background. It is part of my sad case that this repetition of the word Celtic should rouse impatience! Even were I tired of it myself, I should still have to go on, for amongst all drinks whisky alone deals in the colourless logic of truth, permits no other attitude of mind. Perhaps some sort of effort should be made to trace the history of whisky in Scotland and apply it as best one could to the social cataclysms that make Scotland's violent story, from the introduction of Feudalism, through the wars of Independence and of the Covenant, to risings, evictions, and the last housing scheme; but the result would be so much more history than whisky that the true spirit would be certainly drowned. And we are concerned here with the spirit. The real question for us, then, is why should the Scottish mind always have reacted so fiercely, with a fury that England, for example, never achieved—or never had to deplore? What was it in the mind of the people, what was the thwarted or repressed instinct, that made them when driven on the solace of drink not only get drunk, but get beastly drunk; when driven on the slums then to build and inhabit the most abominable in Europe; when driven to protect their faith, then not merely to die for it, but to live and fight for it, with an individual heroism that makes the battle-rush of the Dervishes little more than the whirlwind of an hallucinated fatalism?

It is the fashion to deplore Calvin, and with his logic and its mental tidiness, we may let him rest. But the Covenanters are men first, whose logic may be terrible, but no more terrible than their courage, whose faith is not a religious observance but a whole way of life, whose belief in ultimate individual responsibility was supreme, and who would fight to retain that awful responsibility before God against all the mediating institutions of popes, principalities, and powers. They were the poor common people of Scotland, the tillers of the soil, but they had inherited some tradition that made them rise in their struggle to a spiritual austerity rarely achieved by humanity of any class in any age.

And so we come back to it: what was that tradition?

THE TRADITION

THERE is a book called *The Hidden Ireland*, by Daniel Corkery, which deals with the Irish who lived beyond the Pale in the eighteenth century. It shows, with the impartial historian Lecky, the terrible condition of the peasantry—filth, famine, the plague, and death with the green munge of nettles about its mouth. Outcasts dying off under a penal code which offered no slightest chink of hope to effort howsoever heroic, which denied them land-ownership, the professions, education, their church, with the infamous system of rack-renting tearing them on its wheel. The picture is one of the gloomiest in all history. Then Corkery penetrates beyond Lecky and the other historians and lifts the veil from what is surely one of the most remarkable instances of racial persistence in its highest aspect. For these half-clad, bare-foot, starving peasants inherited a culture from a past so remote that its mythology was as real to them as was Greek mythology to the Athenians. But they not only inherited it, they practised it, and that in its highest manifestation— poetry and music—and found therein their only, their

E   65

last, solace. Were this not sufficiently documented, it were incredible. But there it is, and the author has so lived his theme that with final understanding has come a quietude that rarely rises to a gesture, as though, before what the eyes see and the heart knows, any striving ' to make a case ' would be an adding of the meretricious to the dregs of irony.

There is indeed a wistful note, much as there is in Pater when he writes of Joachim du Bellay and the *Pleiad*; in each of them a lingering preoccupation with, a reiterated insistence upon, the graces and refinements of a perfected technique. For from the immemorial bardic schools of Ireland had come a tradition of poetry written with absolute attention to form and style, to rhythm and harmony; and when these lay universities got broken up by those whom Swift dubbed ' the conquerors ' then the barefoot peasant poets from their fever huts and their stony fields, met in what they called their Courts of Poetry, and there contended with one another, not so much in ' making poetry ' as in improvising variations on a given theme; not as strolling players or simple versifiers, but as masters of language delighting in the artist's use of their medium, in delicate inflections, in subtle assonances, in fleeting gleams and shades, threads of harmony woven into a sound pattern that stole away the senses. Let me give one quotation. When Owen O'Sullivan writes his friend to put a handle in his spade, he couches the request in lyric form; of which a Gaelic verse is Englished:

> ' At the close of day, should my limbs be tired or sore,
>   And the steward gibe that my spade-work is nothing worth,
>   Gently I'll speak of Death's adventurous ways,
>   Or of the Grecian battles in Troy, where princes fell!'

' Labharfad féin go séimh!' (' I myself will gently speak ')—as if he said: ' I will put off the *spailpin*, the earth-delver, and assume my own self, the poet!'

That this should have been going on outside the Pale seems incredible; it reads like a fairy-tale; it is, however, as precisely a matter of fact as the green munge of the nettles. Not only so, but already one observes the introduction of the Renaissance note, with its insidious ' whitening' of the true Gaelic tradition. For the conquering forces were not only destructive, repressive, religiously intolerant, they were also unconsciously the purveyors of the Græco-Roman classicism, or, perhaps more precisely, of that attitude of mind which Pater after his exquisite fashion searched for in his Renaissance essays. The old Gaelic poetry was sun-bred, exuberant and yet vigorous, charged with life or the wild singing of death, positive and challenging. There was a flame at its core. Slowly the flame died down; the red faded to grey; the mind became haunted by dreams; and the inheritors of the ancient rigorous tradition entered, like wraiths, the Celtic Twilight.

Now it may seem fantastic to suggest that apprehension of this is essential to an understanding to-day of what we call the Irish impasse. Yet I believe it to be quite literally true. It is, in fact, the moving truth; that which lies behind economic squabbles, constitutional frameworks, religion, fighting, hate, and blood. For it stands for that integrity and freedom of the mind which, as the Scots said some hundreds of years ago at Arbroath, 'no man gives up but with his life.' And though most of us are prepared to give it up— or (if the euphemism is preferred) not to think about it—yet there are always the few who will stand to it till the heavens fall on them—and on us! Nor does that mean that the Irish in the mass remember the bardic schools or have ever heard of the Courts of Poetry. They do not need to, for the rhythm of that past is in their blood, in the movement of the flesh to prompting instinct, in their indomitable courage, in their drinking and gambling and blasphemy, down even to the very way in which they use the English tongue.

And when I mention the English tongue, I do not refer to quaintnesses of utterance, nor to oddly-phrased translations from the Gaelic, nor even to that living poetic speech so faithfully recorded by Synge in his dramatic dialogue, but to the prose of a figure of such world importance as James Joyce, a prose distinguished above all else by its Irish rhythm, its ' hitherandthithering waters of ' the Gaelic soul.

IN SCOTLAND

THIS excursion into Ireland illumines by reflection the Gaelic spirit in Scotland. In one way it is more dramatic than anything we can offer, for Scotland never suffered directly from a Pale because she was never physically conquered and held. She was often smashed up in parts, of course, as in the period following the '45. And it might suit our purpose, as well as any of a dozen other instances, if we pause for a moment to consider what really did happen after the '45. From his victory at Culloden, Cumberland galloped his dragoons into fiendish atrocities. He seems to have been of opinion that the brutal slaughter of ' savages,' including female and child, was the only sort of salutary lesson applicable to the occasion. We have heard of atrocities, however, since then. Chiefs and others lost their lands, were hanged and quartered, or were lucky enough to flee the country with their lives. All of which they had no doubt been wise enough to anticipate. But it was not until the bloody heat was over that the real thing in the way of destruction began. In 1747 the Government passed an

' Act for securing the peace of the Highlands,' whereby it was ' enacted . . . that no man or boy in that part of Great Britain called Scotland . . . shall on any pretence whatever wear or put on the clothes commonly called Highland clothes . . . and if any such person shall . . .' he got six months for the first offence and, for the second, transportation beyond the seas for the space of seven years.

But the real spirit for Peace is to be found in the oath which the Highlander had to take. He had to swear, as he should answer to God at the last day of Judgment, that he had neither arms nor tartan in his possession, otherwise ' may I be cursed in my undertaking, family, and property—may I never see my wife and children, father, mother, relations—may I be killed in battle as a coward and be without Christian burial in a strange land, far from the graves of my forbears and kindred; may this come across me if I break my oath.'

I feel that no Englishman drafted that oath. It is too diabolical in its insight; shows too searching a knowledge of the very springs of conduct, of the core of the Gaelic spirit. *A coward . . . without Christian burial in a strange land, far from the graves of my forbears and kindred.* Second sight is hardly needed to evoke the tradition behind that.

And in any case, the tradition may quite positively

be found in the music, folk-lore, poetry, and recorded ways of life of the people. ' Collections ' have been made of the last fragments by such as Marjory Kennedy Fraser and Kenneth Macleod in music, by Alexander Carmichael of religious and labour songs and invocations in his beautiful *Carmina Gadelica*, by many others in pipe music (*piobaireachd*), tales (as in Campbell's four volumes), and in variously described delineations of the social life (*ceilidhs*, etc.).

The evidence though fragmentary is overwhelming. And it can be found in other guises. Scotland has long been regarded as the pioneer in education for the common people. The venerable grey-bearded minister, whom I sat under as a boy, was the son of a poor crofter, and as a lad had walked his 250 odd miles to Edinburgh University (starting out with a stone of oatmeal on his back), and, at the end of each session, had walked them back. Respect for learning was so deep-rooted, so profound, that it evoked an emotional response comparable in a certain way with the response to great music. This may be very difficult to understand to-day, but it is nonetheless true.

Presumably such an attitude of mind was not a sudden infliction upon these poor people by an act of God, even allowing, as they were well aware, that their God was a jealous God. With such well-endowed centres of learning and religion already available, as Oxford and Cambridge, it would postulate in the Deity a rather fantastic sense of humour, which would surely have grown a trifle thin by the time it had followed the lad some hundreds of miles on his bare feet, even allowing for divine inscrutability.

Here, then, we come again on the spirit that informed the half-starved peasants in their Courts of Poetry outside the Pale. It is the same spirit, concerned with the things of the mind and excited by them. If we have no recorded evidence of competitions in poetry—we have, as a matter of fact, though it is fragmentary—we certainly have to this day competitions in the ancient music on a high plane. I refer to *piobaireachd*. Some of our Scottish composers are beginning to appreciate the classical form and content of these compositions. 'To the make of a piper,' says Neil Munro, ' go seven years of his own learning and seven generations before.' It is the rigorous note of the old bardic schools.

*   *   *

I agree with the reader who may think that whisky has had very little to do with some of the foregoing pages! Had it had, there would certainly have been a greater lucidity in the writing, a sharper definition of purpose, a more ruthless drive to the Q.E.D. For whisky is rarely tolerant of irrelevances, transfixes the evasive, despises the weak-minded and all those who cannot argue out a case to its irrefutable conclusion. It isolates the human spirit in its native integrity, into its ultimate loneliness, and yet warms that loneliness with creative fire. No adornments, no incense, no rich robes of blessed damozel leaning from the golden bars of an Italian paradise. 'There are two things,' said the Gaelic sage, ' that I like naked, and one of them is whisky.'

Am I implying that all this native tradition of the Scot, this environment of race and time and soil out of which he has come, this inner essence of him, is being denied, frustrated, inhibited (or whatever the word) and that whisky is the liberating agent, the unerring psychoanalyst whose notes for the case-book are gathered at an all-night sitting? Is not the whisky itself taken out of that environment, a dis-tillate of its very spirit? Not a pure spirit—for a pure spirit in the trade is known as a ' silent ' spirit—but a spirit holding in solution those impurities which give it its character, its flavour, and its individuality.

Perhaps we are getting ' warm,' and the drunken-ness of the slums, the austerity of the Covenanters, the dreams of the Twilight, are but efforts to reach out to the lost water of life, so that, being bathed therein, we may at last be revealed to ourselves as we are—and as we know we are. Lemuel's mother advised her son: 'Let him drink and forget his poverty, and remember his misery no more.' There is more humanity and understanding in an odd phrase of the Old Testament, I sometimes think, than in all the uplift books of our modern age.

It looks as if it were going to take us some time yet to get at the making and drinking of the real whisky, but the drier the way the more surely shall we arrive, under the Lord's will! For any Presbyterian who may think that the Lord's will was there invoked wantonly, let me assure him he knows little of how 'the men' of the Scottish Church, when that Church was a more powerful influence in social life than it is to-day, regarded this national drink. 'I very much regret,' wrote Ian Macdonald in an interesting little book called *Smuggling in the Highlands*, to which I am indebted for some historical guidance, 'having to state that the Highland clergy, with one exception, are guilty of the grossest neglect and indifference in this matter (smuggling).' He ardently deplores it. He appeals to the Inverness Gaelic Society to free the Highland people from the stigma of lawlessness, dishonesty, and inevitable demoralization. And he knows what he is writing about. 'Spirits were distilled from the produce of their own lands, and the people being simple and illiterate, ignorant alike of the necessity for a National Exchequer, and of the ways and means taken by Parliament to raise revenue, they could not readily and clearly see the justice of levying a tax upon their whisky. *They drew a sharp distinction between offences created by English statute and violation of the laws of God.*' The italics are mine, as I wished to emphasize the illiteracy and the ignorance.

It was the same ignorance that moved the mind of Alasdair Hutcheson of Kiltarlity, 'worthily regarded as one of the Men of the North.' The Men are the elders, the lay pillars of the Church. Moreover, 'he was not only a pious, godly man, but was meek in spirit and sweet in temper—characteristics not possessed by all men claiming godliness.' But he had inherited the fatal habit of reasoning with himself. 'He had objections to general smuggling,' says Mr Macdonald, 'but argued that he was quite justified in converting the barley grown by himself into whisky to help him to pay the rent of his croft. This he did year after year, making the operation a subject of prayer that he might be protected from the gaugers. One time he sold the whisky to the landlord of the Star Inn, down near the wooden bridge, and arranged to deliver the spirits on a certain night. The innkeeper for some reason informed the local officer, who watched at Clachnaharry until Alasdair arrived about midnight with the whisky carefully concealed in a cart-load of peats. . . . " This is mine," said the officer, seizing the horse's head'. Whereupon Alasdair lifted his face to heaven and cried, ' O Lord, thou hast betrayed me at last ! '

NATIONALISM

THE Celtic background, the tradition we set out to look for, may still seem vague enough, particularly to readers who deplore the introduction through Ireland of the nationalist note! The idea that the Celts should want to establish themselves in an independent nation has something in it at once laughable and monstrous; a presumption so vast that it is grotesque—because haunting the thought of it, like a sniffing dog, is the queer little prehistoric dark shape of fear.

I am quite unable to account for this; I only know that it exists as part of that age-long, and now nearly successful, drive to annihilate all vestiges of the Celt. Any effort on the part of any section—such as Ireland or Wales or Scotland—of the Celtic fringe to form itself into a nation is not merely opposed but bitterly resented as if it were something in the nature of a betrayal of human progress. This is pure mystery and therefore curiously moving. And I am not implying here that this mystical opposition is confined to politicians or ordinary citizens; on the contrary, it is to be found in its greatest strength in writers like Mr H. G. Wells, who fascinate themselves and others by fitting puzzling manifestations of the human spirit into a nice all-inclusive jigsaw-pattern of the world's maw. Even their very axioms are suspect. Let us consider—at the risk of making too long an excursion—their fundamental one : nationalism is the cause of war.

I have been unable to find any argument to prove to me that nationalism is the cause of war. Nationalism is an instrument that war uses, of course, but then so is the bagpipe. If any English pacificist said to me that bagpipes should be destroyed in the interests of international peace, I should hesitate to agree with him, even though able to follow the profounder intricacies of his anxiety. Nor would it, I hope, occur to me to counter him by tentatively suggesting the abolition of the brass band, for the instrument within the glittering ensemble that says pom-pom-*pom*, does so after a fashion that suggests a fateful rather than a martial note. However, I am ignorant and illiterate in all matters pertaining to brass bands, and merely surmise that even an Englishman who had never been to the Crystal Palace finals would yet hesitate over so drastic a step as total prohibition of the brass band in the interests of universal harmony.

What, then, causes war?

Supposing I answered that war as we know it

to-day is a result of economic unreason, I believe I should be fairly dead on the mark. Imagine, for a moment, what the world would be like if there was no unemployment as we understand that term, no poverty in the midst of plenty, no fear of starvation and all the jealousies and hates bred out of fear, no ultimate power in the hands of a few international financiers, no private control of armament firms whose dividends come out of war. Does the ordinary Englishman *want* to kill a Russian or a German or a Frenchman, because each of these gentlemen belongs to a different nation? Not a bit of it. The thing is against human nature. You hit a man on the jaw who annoys you on the street or in the House of Commons, but you are not *naturally* moved to murder someone across the sea whose very existence you accept on faith. You do not rob your neighbour's house if you have sufficient sustenance in your own; nor could any argument, nationalist or other, work you up to the indignity of raiding his larder. But immediately you are both liable to starve, and therefore both anxious to grab what you can at home and abroad, then the selfish powers that should have solved your economic problem protect themselves from your wrath by making you fight each other. The world is overstocked with all the good things man has grown and manufactured for his own use, yet he is not allowed to enjoy them. Indeed rather than allow him, the controlling powers destroy vast quantities of them annually, and have now set out on a policy of restricting their creation—solemnly, ' to keep up the price '! I used the expression ' economic unreason.' There is, however, a mad reason in it—the madness that leads through discontent and starvation and wrought-up nerves to inevitable war.

Now if this comes near the truth, how despicable a thing it is to saddle nationalism with the total blame! Despicable, because nationalism stands for the ultimate integrity of a people, and the expression in the arts and the applied arts of that which gives them their greatest delight. Nationalism can be used for war, precisely as Christianity was used for war, but no one now suggests that war is implicit in the doctrines of the Prince of Peace! It is the old game of finding something or someone to blame for a state of affairs we are ashamed, or too cowardly, to look in the face.

All this crying for less nationalism and more internationalism is the vague sentimentality of an age decorated by leaders whose economic conceptions are necessarily (or they would be bad business men) predatory, and troubled to the point of despair by popular thinkers who desire to ease their mental indigestion into the godhead of Size, who forget the individual—the only moral responsibility real to us—in yearning for the mass, and its mass production.

It is as though the most earnest of them cried let the chanter be more like the harp, the harp tune in to the trombone, the trombone communicate its trouble to the violin, the violin deepen sympathetically towards the 'cello . . . so that we may have a real international orchestra. Though, of course, it is only when each instrument is most exquisitely true to itself that the highest orchestral harmony is achieved.

Or let us look at the only modern experiment in solving this economic unreason: Russian communism. The idea in communism is that what is produced in common shall be consumed in common, and towards that end ownership in production and distribution shall be held in common. Now whether we think that a bad or a good idea, it represents a fairly logical effort to defeat the existing unreason, with its artificial un-employment and ' poverty amidst plenty.'

But, in the first place, when Lenin set out on his logical effort, he did not say to himself, It is impossible for me ever to right this hideous misery in one nation without first of all having all the other nations in harmony with me. He was not overcome by senti-mental aspiration. He knew that all great things had come from individual peoples or nations, just as all

great ideas come from individual men. Ancient
Greece and her Greeks; Judæa and Christ. Nor was
he greatly concerned with the vehement dreams of
red Internationals: the obverse to the inflated essentially Fascistic Clissoldism. Being a realist, Lenin
first set about realizing his idea in his own country.
He knew the Carlylean concept: if a man has a zeal
for reform let him reform himself first and there
will be one rascal the less in the world. And so with
the nation.

His experiment is still being worked out. Last year
when Stalin, his successor, met H. G. Wells, the
creator of Clissold, and they conversed in a manner
that Mr Wells reported, George Bernard Shaw sum-
marized the talk in a witty analysis of the Wellsian
viewpoint. 'Here is Russia solving all the problems
which we are helplessly trying to buy off with doles,
to frighten off with armaments, and to charm away
with prayers for a revival of trade. In the course of
solving them, political discoveries in applied political
science of the most thrilling interest and vital importance have been made,' writes Mr Shaw; and he then
proceeds to describe how Mr Wells 'trotted into the
Kremlin and said, in effect, "Mr Stalin, you are a
second-rate person with your second-rate head stuffed
with a piece of nonsense called the Class War, which
my friends in the P.E.N. Club would not listen to

for a moment. Now listen to me whilst I explain to you the vast possibilities of The World of William Clissold, etc., etc., etc." ' Mr Bernard Shaw makes very amusing comedy out of it all, for he realizes precisely the importance of what is being actually done in Russia. And in trying to make clear to Mr Wells the grounds on which Stalin's leadership is founded, he begins : ' First, he is a practical Nationalist statesman recognizing that Russia is a big enough handful for mortal rulers to tackle without taking on the rest of the world as well (Wells will have nothing short of a World State).'

Now the point for us here is that Russia believes she has solved the economic riddle; and, so believing, she at once adopts the attitude of encouraging the various nationalisms within her own borders. She even officially calls herself the Union of Socialist Soviet Republics. Manifestly neither Lenin nor Stalin believed that nationalism of itself is a cause of war. They were not at all likely to create that which would interfere internally with the working of their stupendous experiment; on the contrary, they would create only that which would assist materially and spiritually towards its most rapid and most efficient consummation. In short, whenever the economic irritant is removed, nationalism stands for healthy growth. (Lest any reader thinks the foregoing an insidious effort at disseminating Communism, may I say in the by-going that there is one other plan I should like to try first. The author of it, however, is named Douglas, and I should not like to jeopardize his scheme in the tiniest degree by mentioning his nationality.)

What I am getting at in all this is, I believe, of grave importance. It might be put in the form of a rhetorical question: Are we, in panic fear of war, to discredit the distinctions and differences that make life varied and complex and inexhaustibly fascinating in order to follow the demagogues who babble of some universal Euclidean agreement, so that any one life placed on any other will coincide with it in all respects? How appalling the prospect! Like those ' scientific ' pictures of the future with human beings living and working in congeries of beehives, pale as wax and as aseptic, dominated by an order that denies the individual intellect for the satisfaction of the common belly. With how suffocating a nightmare does this economic unreason ride us!

Nationalism has, of course, its Fascists and other jingoists who debase it from the spiritual thing it is to a shirt-and-baton parade at the best and, at the worst, to a bloody lust. Nor need Clissold try to rub that home, for Hitler and Clissold under their skins bear the same relationship to each other as did the Colonel's lady to Judy O'Grady. Only there was this to be said for Hitler in the beginning, that he was the bellicose beacon thrown up by a people who would not allow their spirit to be indefinitely done down. When a man (or nation) is attacked in his last citadel, his response is not always pretty. Ordinarily he will fight or plot or get bestially drunk. Extraordinarily he will face up to crucifixion or hemlock, for domination or torture here is not enough, inasmuch as, of the truth that is in him, he will say to his last breath, ' It moves.'

Only the sentimentalist, with every good intention in the world, would have suggested to Jesus that he might have postponed the Sermon on the Mount until the rabbinical weather had cleared up a bit, or to Socrates that he should have gone more warily about his truth-hunt, or kindlily—torture irons are nasty things—to Galileo that it did not matter so awfully much, did it really, whether the earth moved or not.

It may be unfortunate that individual and national souls exist, and some day we may be able to dispense with both. But meantime it is surely too radical a remedy to suggest, for instance, not the removal of Hitlerism but the destruction of the German soul. I know a lady who because she really loves her garden and her roses works without gloves. Surely it would be a trifle extreme—however logical—to suggest to her that the cutest way of avoiding thorn-pricks would be by cutting off her hands. She could no doubt aim at getting the roses pruned by machinery. It is granted completely, but I am not concerned with that; I am only concerned with the fact *that she loves to prune the roses herself.* And I am fairly confident that it is out of that love—and that love alone—that roses come.

THE INTERNATIONAL CUP

But let us get back to whisky for the final argument.

Whisky came out of and continues to come out of Scotland and Ireland. England does pretty well with her beer. The one memorable thing that my mind has carried through the years from Saintsbury's *Notes on a Cellar Book* is the label that had been affixed to a barrel of beer and inscribed: ' Mr George Saintsbury. Full to the bung.' In that serious work, Saintsbury included, of course, some notes on whisky—as well he might, for did he not begin his Cellar Book in Elgin, which is a city in its own ancient right, and, more important, the capital of the kingdom of whisky? There is a robustiousness about that great soul, a fullness-to-the-bung, that is forever England. What beer lacks in concentrated power it makes up with a great copiousness. It is a deluge of a drink. I once knew a man who in the course of an evening consumed eighteen pints, and then had a final one by way of friendly good-night.

If an urge comes on me to dwell on beer with its human warmths and heroic bellies, perhaps it is by way of unconscious contrast to the attitude of M. Crémieux, who could not easily forget the charge of the bourgeois Scottish intellectuals towards the whisky and sherry. (I hear a certain gargantuan laughter dying off.) But M. Crémieux goes on to say, ' This violent taste for alcohol which begins beyond the frontiers of France always remains rather mysterious to a Frenchman from south of the Loire, where people drink brandy and *fine champagne* much as they smell a flower.' How superb, how exquisite an utterance is that! The fragrance rises from within the frontiers of France like the bouquet from the rim of a glass. How perfect, how lovely a nationalism!

And if we could find a Portuguese Crémieux writing on port, is it conceivable—appalling thought! —that the palate of Mr Galsworthy's English Stoic might be deemed by him to be, how shall one say? a trifle fruity, and even that Saintsbury was in his calmer moments, in his subtler appreciations, still inclined to a northern robustiousness, a climatic tolerance, that hazed the vision of the true flower?

Perhaps there are Spaniards who died on first hearing of sherry-and-bitters.

But I am being led away—drink is the great adventurer—from my immediate business which was to concoct a true international drink, one that would at

once satisfy the charging Scot, the charged Englishman, the flower-fragrant Frenchman, the Italy of
salutation, the Spain of courtesy, the Russia of adventure; that would consummate the noble aspirations
of Clissold, ameliorate the temper of Hitler, and meet
fairly and squarely the requirements of the Esperant-
ists. A universal Cup of Peace; or as Burns so humanly
put it, a Cup of Kindness Yet. There is every excuse
for excitement here.

Into this Cup then, first and foremost, equal measures
of The Glenlivet and John Jameson, matured for ten
years in sherry wood—first, because through all the
fragrances of the world the Celtic spirit will arise like
a forgotten incense. Add beer—a noble measure,
drawn from the wood so that it be still and freed
from the Imperial gasses. Next a true wine of the
Loire, one of those tranquil wines, quiet as a flower
in a calm air. M. Crémieux makes me feel my
ignorance with his brandy and *fine champagne*. For
I had thought of the Loire otherwise, and indeed had
journeyed amongst its vineyards with different quest
and intent. But brandy most certainly; though it
is not a wine but a distillate of wine, a spirit of wine,
and thus acts upon the same plane as the spirit of the
barley. But how differently! For the barley is
wholesome and quick in body and brain, dispelling
the vapours, abolishing gloom, flashing its light to

the last bourne. Brandy is insidious; its false security lures the spirit to forgetfulness; it is Sin without its weariness; it is the water of death. It is used to fortify wine for the English palate. For in true wine there is no sin. Into the cup, then, pour the brandy. And lest we become thoughtful, add at once a champagne whose bubbles will wink us to laughter. Stir. Where is the Portuguese who doubted the great Saintsbury? Let him prove himself. And the Spaniard from Xerxes? Ha, noble Signor, in with it! And who is this bearing a wine nearly as black as his shirt? The Roman. And this wine clearer than the river of the Lorelei, swung from a brown swastika? . . .

The Cup is full.

The great moment has arrived.

Always France has held Europe in thrall. The pale face of her son, with its black beard and clear forehead, approaches. The nostrils quiver at the brim. A faint convulsion—and the face draws back.

' Is it this universal drink of Peace,' cries Clissold, tubby in his person but splendidly anxious in his soul, ' or is it War? '

Gallantly the Frenchman returns to the Cup. He sips, and over his features passes a deathly pallor as if of hemlock he had drunk.

' Peace—or War? ' cries Clissold.

But the price is too great.
' *Messieurs, c'est la guerre.*'

★   ★   ★

If I appear to be fighting hard for whisky and its
Celtic background, it is because I believe I have a
good cause and a noble drink. The tendency to size,
to mass production, to uniformity, is surely bad in
a moral sense. The destruction of variety is the
creation of apathy, sameness breeds boredom and
sloth. It may seem oracular to say that modern
machinery is annihilating space and time and therefore all distinctions between peoples. It is just about
as oracular—or as idiotic—as to say that psychology
is abolishing all differences between individuals, or
that Freud has emptied our mental asylums. Only
the rich maniac keeps forever travelling—in some
infernal effort to avoid his own eyes. The scientist
has his laboratory fixed, requires time and solitude
for that close concentration which alone permits his
individual intelligence to move step by step to the
boundary of knowledge, and then, with infinite and
exhausting labour, to attempt its one small step beyond.
The thinker, the poet, requires the same solitude, but
has to be rooted more firmly, because it is out of the
root he draws the sap of life with its dark currents.
There has never been a cosmopolitan poet of the first

greatness, because cosmopolitanism has no root, no tradition. Perhaps, fundamentally, it is given to a man to know one thing and to observe many.

But supposing that is all wrong, and that when economic unreason has been resolved every being on earth will have access to flying machines, luxury liners, and all the rest of it, what about any silly antiquated ideas of nationalism then?

Personally I may say that when deck bowls started for the third week on board the luxury liner, I was not thrilled. At the end of a further three weeks, I could conceive myself giving the promenade the slip for Mr Eliot's Waste Land, prepared to find agreeable change in betting on the vagaries of Sweeney's nightingale rather than on the nautical miles the ship had logged. When the pastime of gadding-about has become universal, some restless poet will use it for adding another ring to the classical Inferno. Then to go out into the desert may socially become the thing to do—or at any rate, to find a spot that is for ever England. Only the philosophers and poets would make for the desert. Can it be that Scotland, which is being turned into a desert with alarming rapidity, has this destiny in front of her, that the cairngorm will become the philosopher's stone? The ways of destiny are inscrutable—and any day now they may turn from a preoccupation with conquering

to the art of civilizing. Scotland has never yet led
the world as Greece did or Venice. Is her time coming
at last when in face of a world given over to mass
emotion and mass thought, to strident Fascism,
religious Communism, self-heating Clissoldism, she
will assert once more individual responsibility and
the individual soul? She has the tradition. She has
the water of life. How fascinating it would be to
watch her take hold of herself and set out on the great
enterprise! I know there are English and Scots, sound
Empire-men, who go solemnly pale at the notion: a
thoughtful instance of the oddity of cosmic humour.

*　　*　　*

If I am not quite done with this aspect of the argument, blame drink. I have by me a *Book of French
Wines* (by P. Morton Shand) whose opening words
run: ' France is, as Redding, who himself enumerated
some 1600 French wines, said, "the vineyard of the
earth" . . .'

I think that almost parenthetic reference to 1600
different wines holds a great lesson. All my Presbyterian instincts stir in me. The fruits of the earth,
the vineyard in parable, the miracle of turning the
water into wine, the bountifulness of the Giver, the
whole marvel of Creation. How noble a complexity,
how intricate a design, how inexhaustible a resource!

That I shall never know a tithe of the 1600 induces not despair but, I should like to think, the true philosophic humility. For—the adventure is ever open. If Mr Morton Shand should magically appear and, after referring to the public gentlemen who talk of uniformity and universality, because they fear complexity and difference, who forever have their eyes in the ends of the earth because, as the Bible says, they are fools, invite me to accompany him, first having prepared myself as for a festival, on a journey through the 'vineyard of the earth' (his own opening sentence was finely complicated), should I remind him as we went companionably on our way that in the preface to his sound work he wrote that it was his 'firm belief that the only effective defence against agitations designed to enforce Prohibition in Great Britain lies in fostering true Temperance by increasing the consumption of natural wines and decreasing that of spirits'? I should not. I should forgive him, I hope, silently.

Even as I hope to forgive M. Crémieux and other gentlemen from foreign parts. They have been acted upon by music-hall caricatures, and, in any case, were predisposed by some inscrutable destiny to deny and exterminate the Celt. As I, too, may be forgiven in my turn for suggesting the remote possibility that the Scot, despite his traducers, is the least provincial of all men. I cannot readily imagine a Scot of the eminence of M. Crémieux having quite the same sincerity of utterance in recording an impression of the French. As in Dunne's *Serial Universe*, the Scot would be inclined to look at himself as he gave such an impression, then to look at himself looking at himself. . . . It is so difficult, once the terms of the simple series to infinity have been grasped, to perform perfectly the act of condescension.

I gather that Mr Dunne was helped to his mathematical demonstration of our mind's immortality by a close study of prevision—the sort of 'second sight' which has hitherto been regarded merely as one of the grosser superstitions of the Gael, and which I have heard deplored as a devilish traffic of the mind akin, on the physical plane, to illicit distillation.

The Scot has never stereotyped a caricature of anyone, even of his neighbour with whom he quarrelled for so many centuries. This is a fact. Possibly a sad one. And when the English smile at how the Scot is supposed to boast of his Scottishness, it should be remembered—not only for the light it casts on the Scot.

The French critic is as helpful as any Englishman. We perceive in his smiling sincerity that perfect self-assurance, that inner conviction of reality, which permits an utterance of instruction. For in his smile there is no conscious condescension—and this, to the Scot, is so superb a fact that his dry irony fades before it into profound metaphysical contemplation.

In this contemplation the foreign smile may be seen disembodied as the smile of the Cheshire cat, and its mercilessness achieves immortality as a perfect abstraction.

*　　*　　*

Perhaps all this may have the air of ' heavy going,' or possibly resemble one of those refinements of the peasant poets of the Courts of Poetry! They say it is difficult for the leopard to change his spots. And perhaps the modern Scot, when bred from his true background, is inclined to come all over Gaelic spots in a sort of traditional rash or fever at the most inconvenient moments. The English do it with their own pink spots consistently and with dignity—with all the dignity, say, of Mr Baldwin discoursing on St. George, with unheard roll of drums and pervasive Rule Britannia, off. Though that, impressive as it is, is not the real England, the England of ' This England.' No Englishman but is thrilled with ' This England,' quietly, keeping his head, like an assured lover.

> ' Oh, to be in England
> Now that April's there . . .'

How the spots run into a delicate flush! One thinks of Rupert Brooke, tree foliage and green lawns, the smooth cheeks of young women, woods and afternoon tea in cities, and no slums.

> ' If I should die, think only this of me :
> That there's some corner of a foreign field
> That is for ever England . . .'

No Scots irony may resolve that into a music-hall impertinence. It remains simple and splendid. It leads me, anyway, to shy salutation.

We cannot parallel its simplicity in Scotland.

The nearest approach to this bright positive reality of love is perhaps :

> ' From the dim shieling and the misty island
> Mountains divide us and a world of seas . . .'

The note of nostalgia, of separation, of the past. In all things pertaining to his land that move the Scot to his marrow you will observe this note of tragedy, this singing of lost causes, of dead years, of death.

Are we back at the old Celtic background again? At the race that is fated to die ; at the race that long ago brewed its own death potion and with disintegrating irony (still characteristic of the Scot) called it the ' water of life ' ?

HIGHLANDS AND LOWLANDS

I HEAR a voice: 'What about the Lowlands? Half our population is in the Clyde valley and when it yells "Come away the Celtic!" it doesn't mean what you mean.'

Possibly. If only I knew what I meant myself!

Yet I am more than half convinced that in my argument the moving finger writes, however dimly. When we take the long perspective of history there appears to be a steady progress from the savage to Einstein. We can hardly doubt the increase in profundity and power of the human mind. Yet when any particular section of the 'steady progress' is taken, how the pendulum seems to swing backward as well as forward! Rise and fall; power and decadence. But Einstein emerges.

And even when Einstein is cast out by the German people, the cause, if we could see deeply enough, might be quite other than we suspect. After the war, German youth was seized by a great idealism, nothing less than to build a new and holy nation as a salute to their dead. All thought of another war was repudiated. Freedom was to be 'born again' in the western world. Like proud crusaders they bore the title 'Youth Movement.' There was indeed all the religious feeling of a crusade. How it all walked the treadmill of the Social Democrats (Ebert and the rest of the tired older generation) until it met Hitler, born of Versailles, is the stuff of great tragedy. But that it still exists, that 'liberty' and 'brotherhood,' the twin terms of historic German idealism, are alive in the young German heart to-day, I believe quite simply. We have reached neither the end of Einstein nor of German idealism. When Hitler goes Einstein will return. That is all we can be sure of. The rest is the smoke that obscures the everlasting fire.

So, too, when we return to Scotland and our question. In his book, *The Heart of Scotland*, Mr George Blake shows us Scotland as he finds her, without mitigating the ruthlessness of his picture in any way. It is a sincere and cogent piece of work. Yet when I try to resolve some of his problems I find that what he has observed sometimes leaves contradiction beneath. For example, he draws the usual line between Highlands and Lowlands and says, 'It is a country of two races, one mainly Celtic and one mainly Teuton.' But a page or so further on he writes, ' All Britain felt the force of the Reformation —and England made out of it the charming and

characteristic compromise of Episcopalianism. When
Scotland was infected it had to be all or nothing—
and the result was Calvinism unadulterated, if not
a little intensified.'

Why didn't the Teutonic Lowlands show the same
charming reaction as Teutonic England? Actually
Highlands and Lowlands behaved alike, striving for
the same end with the same fury, the *furor caledoniensis*
or *perfervidjum scotorum* of historic Scotland. Accordingly—for nothing moves the spirit more profoundly
than religious feeling—I am compelled to conclude
that spiritually the Highlands and Lowlands are akin
over against England, and not England and the
Lowlands over against the Highlands. The difference which Mr Blake observed is, I feel, essentially
superficial, such a difference in the main as will be
found between a desperate industrialism and an
ancient agrarianism existing side by side amongst any
people. Your Catholic-Orange fight is a Celtic fight,
a Celtic fury. England takes no part, probably
regarding the whole thing as barbaric—and probably
rightly. But I am not concerned with any kind or
manifestation of religion here but with some attempt
at isolating and recognizing that temper of a people
which will show through all they profess, whether in
the *form* of barbarism, defeatism, or whisky-drinking.

Let us agree, with the French savant, that the Celts

were not conquerors but merely civilizers. Let us admit at the same time that the English have been conquerors, and we begin to perceive how when they say to the Irish we will *give* you this or that part of your freedom, they are genuinely astonished when the Irish are not satisfied, nay, they are sincerely hurt in the generosity—that has been compelled from them. When all our miserable squabbles are resolved, this will remain, for purposes of ironic humour, the most humourless business in all history. The Scots have long been regarded as lacking in humour, as requiring a surgical operation to perceive a joke. Now I observe the inspired British press is turning the same weapon on their erstwhile humorous Irish by calling a certain leader a ' humourless pedant.' I do not even require to mention his name. Already the caricature is being stereotyped. The process is *en train*.

And if honest British citizens will blame me for this excursion, the best I can plead is the Scot's partiality for a dryness in the flavour. This prolonged concern with whisky and the Celtic background must be given its moment of indulgence. I promise from now on to stick to Scotland.

*　　*　　*

This dividing of Scotland, then, into two separate countries, separate peoples, called Highland and Lowland, is a practice of considerable antiquity, founded on the principle: Divide and destroy. When Mr Evan M. Barron, in his original study, *The Scottish War of Independence*, began to enquire into the matter, he found that the first thing he had to do was to expose the untruth in the work of previous historians, like Lang, who had said that the Scottish War of Independence was a war of Anglo-Saxon against Anglo-Saxon. Mr Barron showed, on the other hand, that the Lothians were not concerned with the initiation or progress of the struggle, which was one of Celtic Scotland against Anglo-Saxon England. He demonstrates how it started in the north, swept westward and south, until the Highlanders under Moray joined forces with the Lowland Celts under Wallace (Gaelic was still being spoken in Galloway a hundred odd years ago). His case is so clearly documented that no one has dared challenge it since it first appeared some twenty years ago. And the profound thing in it is also the obvious, namely, that being a Celtic struggle it was therefore a struggle by the commons of Scotland. It was not a feudal lord's war of aggrandizement; it was a passionate fight by the people of Scotland for their country's freedom. That is the Scotland on which we found, and I know of no argument that can gainsay it.

I have a memory of Tolstoi's saying somewhere

that Napoleon went muttering uneasily of ' England and her gold ' as if he were being pursued by a ghost. England early developed that power of getting others to fight for her or, more subtly, of causing her enemies at critical moments to fall out and fight one another. The strategy has been applied to Scotland with slow, cumulative, remorseless effect—right from the first introduction of feudalism, through the Covenanting period, the Jacobite risings, up to even so recent a barbarity as the ' Clearances,' when the Sutherland glens were overawed by a regiment of Irish foot, who came muttering of the damned Highlanders—who had been sent to fight them in Ireland. I have already mentioned the ' Highland Host ' that was imposed on Ayrshire. What a hatred of the tartan must have been generated there! How the very idea of the Highlands must have stunk in the nostrils of the Lowlander! For that and other reasons, there are Lowlanders to this day who dislike and deride the Highlanders, feel different from them and jeer at them. And there are Highlanders who would rather have direct government contact with London than with Edinburgh or Glasgow. The wars, the Bannockburns and Floddens, the savagery to Wallace or the townspeople of Berwick, the bloody forays into Northumberland, all can be forgotten or remembered with a smile, but this insidious dividing of Scotland has been a poison working in her system to this day and it is difficult to forgive the strategy that introduced it, not for anything diabolic or otherwise in the strategy itself, but because in this particular instance it resulted in the disintegration of a nation, and to that extent destroyed whatever national contribution it might have made to the enriching of international life and the leading of humanity away from its crude preoccupation with war and conquest to that consideration and enhancement of those *things of the spirit* which alone differentiate us from the brutes. Perhaps here at last may be found my only excuse for having been concerned so long with the Celtic background.

And here at last also I am prepared to make a strange admission, namely that I do not much mind whether it is called Celtic or not. I am well aware there is no such thing as racial purity in any nation. It is possible, indeed certain, that a strong underlying strain in the Scot is pre-Celtic. One could ask questions and propound theories to fill a larger book than this. Personally, I find the word Pictish very attractive! But all in all, we can have a fairly clear picture of the common people of Scotland from early times, their drink, their habits, their arts, their dreams, their fun, their bestial lapses and heroic moments. We know of their systems of land tenure and social organization—so opposed in basic principle to the feudal system that was insidiously but inexorably—if never completely successfully—imposed upon them.

For the rest, an attitude of unconcern is conceivable towards any disillusioned Scot who may desire to take the Anglo-Norman clan chiefs, the Anglo-Scottish nobility, the Bonnie Prince Charlies, and all of the ' romance ' that goes with them, and drop the whole tinsel-glittering or blood-glittering box of toys in the Thames. Though that was hardly worth saying inasmuch as whatever may have been valid in them was, by their own aspiration, drowned in the Thames long ago. With rare exceptions, the nobles and clan chiefs of Scotland, in the tragic hours of their people's need, showed themselves the sorriest and most treacherous crew that ever a decent land was damned by.

*　　　*　　　*

Let us get back to whisky for finality.

With a view, it was said, to facilitating the collection of the duty on whisky, Scotland in 1787 was divided by Act of Parliament into Lowland and Highland districts. In the Highland district duty was not to continue to be charged, as in the Lowlands and England, on the gallon of spirits, but on the capacity of the still. For this purpose the Highland line was carefully plotted in the Act, and it may be interesting here to give its main points: ' A certain line or boundary beginning at the east point of Loch Crinan . . . Loch Gilpin . . . Inveraray, Arrochar, Tarbet, north side of Ben Lomond, Callendar, Crieff, Dunkeld . . . Fettercairn, . . . Clatt, Huntly, Keith, Fochabers . . . Elgin and Forres, to the boat on the river Findhorn. . . .'

This measure caused the greatest confusion. It was assumed that a still could produce, for each gallon of its capacity, a certain quantity per annum, so the only concern of the Revenue was to ensure that no existing still was enlarged or new still set up without due notice. Highland distillers have always, however, been acute business men. By improving their stills, they contrived to reduce the time taken to work off a charge from the normal one week—to eight minutes! The authorities, of course, considered this ' sharp practice,' got immediately on the hunt and raised the duty from £1, 4s. per gallon content to nearly £8, plus additional duty on the actual gallons made. To keep ahead, the distiller had to get quantity at all costs and certainly at the cost of quality, with the natural result that a demand struck up for the illicit and better product. Smuggling increased. The Government grew desperate, and in 1814 prohibited

the use of stills of a less capacity than 500 gallons—
thus compelling the Highlander, who must have his
dram, to illicit distillation.

Colonel Stewart of Garth, an acute observer, wrote
of this new Act: 'It was evident that this law was
a complete interdict, as a still of this magnitude would
consume more than the disposable grain in the most
extensive county within this newly drawn boundary;
nor could fuel be obtained for such an establishment
without an expense which the community could not
possibly bear. The sale, too, of the spirits produced
was circumscribed within the same line, and thus the
market which alone could have supported the manufacture was entirely cut off.'

That last sentence shows how neat was the check-
mate. The Highlanders were privileged to pay duty
on a whisky they could make only for their own
use, but always on condition that they made it in
a pot so large that they could neither afford to buy
nor fill it.

But we have learned these last few years how the
Highland farmer is hit when the Highland distiller
is hit. It was exactly the same in 1814, when the
farmers could not sell their surplus barley 'in any
manner adequate to pay rents.' Thus for the Highlands 'hardly any alternative remained,' wrote Colonel
Stewart, 'but that of having recourse to illicit dis-

tillation, or resignation of their farms and breach of their engagements with their landlords. These are difficulties of which the Highlanders complain heavily, asserting that nature and the distilling laws present unsurmountable obstacles to the carrying on of a legal traffic.' The gallant Colonel concludes: 'If it be indeed true that the illegal traffic has made such deplorable breaches in the honesty and morals of the people, the revenue drawn from the large distilleries, to which the Highlanders have been made the sacrifice, has been procured at too high a price for the country.'

The Government was obviously more frightened of the Highlands in those days than in these. In 1815 the distinction between Highlands and Lowlands, in the matter of whisky duty, was graciously discontinued.

'Drunkenness,' says M. Hubert, 'was a failing of the Celts.' But he provides an even better clue to the identity of Highlands and Lowlands than that. He shows that literature was popular amongst the common people, the Celtic folk, in a way that could not be paralleled in other races; and thus we immediately understand not merely the Gaelic poets of the Isles, like Mary Macleod, but the 'Doric' poets of the Lowlands, like Robert Burns. 'The Celtic epic showed a feeling for heroic poetry, a sense of the marvellous, mingled with humour, and a dramatic conception of fatality which truly belong to the Celts alone.' One might find other words for describing the Lowland Hugh McDiarmid's *A Drunk Man Looks at the Thistle*, but it would be difficult to be more apt in the same space. This is not only an arresting fact, but one charged with great illumination. Instances could be adduced almost without end. Think of Burns, his dramatic instinct for the marvellous, his satire charged not with bitterness but with laughter, his addresses to death, to whisky, his drinking bouts, his hellsbells ride with Tam o' Shanter at midnight, the human warmth and depth of the man that gave to his simplest lyrical passage the reality of profound utterance. Burns does not express the whole matter, any more than does Mary Macleod or Alexander Macdonald or Carlyle (what a fury was there!) or Hugh McDiarmid or others, differing from one another intensely as individuals, but manifestly coming out of the same tradition and belonging, if one must have it, to the same School, or to the same Spirit, or even to the same spirits. 'Freedom and whisky gang thegither,' said Burns, with the poet's high gift of showing the range of his human experience in the pure vision of a few words. Poverty, social injustice, degradation—the memory of so vast an impertinence has to be drowned before the soul may rise into freedom and breathe its native air and eject its spittle

of laughter on what are still designated in the feu-
charters of our lives as ' superiors.'

> ' A king can mak a belted knight,
> A marquis, duke, and a' that.'

Quite clearly Burns, though a Lowlander, has never
taken to the feudal system, any more than the crofters
of the Highlands who kept on fighting the alien
enslavement until they gave it at least a partial check
by forcing the Government to pass a Crofter's Act
embodying the ancient right of ' security of tenure.'

And if all that appears to give the spirit only a
certain strength or violence, then it is one-sided, for
in no poetry, peasant or otherwise, may be found a
truer evocation of human tenderness and love ; which,
indeed, any psychologist would expect, for always in
the heart of native strength there is a core of tenderness. When the strength is sapped the tenderness
loses its direction, spreads out and grows shallow ;
like a stream that has lost its channel, it waters whatever weeds, briar bushes, or cabbage patches come
in its way, producing among them for a little time a
sentimental flush of life.

The Kailyaird School thus derives directly from the
ancient Celtic source. The love of learning, for
example, is in it to a marked degree, is in fact its
chief ornament. It smoothes the skin of its characters

to a refinement that is phthisical. It is in essence the epic of the peasant's son who instead of becoming a poet becomes a university professor and returns from that inhuman struggle to die of consumption amongst the cabbages when the briars are in bloom. There is loose talk of Fiona Macleod, and other talk of ladies and gentlemen in tartan who frequent the Outer Isles, listening for the song of the seal or squatting on lonely islands sublimating what their southern hearts may whisper of defeat, as the begetters of the Celtic twilight. Another whisky to drown the memory of *that* impertinence! If not in fact, still in spirit, Scotland is a nation, and the Kailyaird School is her true Celtic Twilight.

Nor is there any use deploring or damning the fact, or, by a natural if essentially weak reaction, rushing into ecstatic descriptions of fornication in the gutter to exhibit our emancipation from it. Unreal, sentimental, sterile, with the rose-flush of death on its face, the Kailyaird may have been, but it carried over in its fashion the love of learning, the desire for refinements, and has somewhere in it, like a fever, the craving for the primordial goodness that civilization crushed so long ago.

* * *

I am aware that any effort to show the 'spirit of a people' even through its literature can give rise to unending argument. Deviations from the norm, personal prejudice, a finical concern for trivialities, any of a hundred and one irritants will keep discussion going for long enough. There is one fairly remorseless test, however, and it may be found in the institutions a people or nation has created.

Mr Innes of Learney recently provided a basic contrast when he showed that the folk in Scotland are divided vertically and in England horizontally. The clan consisted of individuals to whom the idea of arranging themselves in social layers simply could not occur. Here we have in essence the distinction between the ancient clan system and the feudal system. And all the institutions Scotland has created have embodied in them this vertical conception of individualism and democracy. Even when she set about reforming her Church, she did it in characteristic fashion, and left it to be governed not by any hierarchy but by lay members of each congregation. The minister himself could be ' had up ' before the Session. I am not concerned here with whether this is a better or worse form of Church government than the Anglican or Roman, I am merely trying to face the fact that it is a democratic and not a hieratic or autocratic one. Nor need I consider whether I have been using the terms clan system and feudalism loosely inasmuch as clan chiefs became feudal lords. They did—but the

men and women of the clans have never in their
bones recognized the change, as their outcries at the
time of the evictions showed, and as their fight in
the wild days of the land leaguers (compare the fight
in Ireland) proved.

Church, education, law, special creations like the
Convention of Royal Burghs—instances may be
gathered from any institutional growth of the people's
will.

Compared with the English, we appear to come
out of a different spiritual and physical background.
Again, let me say, it may be a poorer, less interesting
background ; or again, it may not ; but it is different.
And I have a notion that it is these differences, however much or little in kind or degree, that make life
fascinating, capable of infinite permutation and com-
bination, of design, of beauty, of endowing us, by
powers of comparison, with that understanding which
now and then imagines it glimpses the creative purpose
of the Grand Architect, the President of the Immortals,
the Unknown God.

Now if this physical and spiritual background is a reality, then we should expect to find some evidence of its active existence in Scotland, as in Ireland and Wales.

Of Ireland I have said enough. Of Wales, where the Celtic tongue has still a natural life, I should merely like to say that once I listened in to an English lord, in a discussion with a Welshman on the subject of Welsh autonomy, referring slightingly to the figures of the Eisteddfod as ' clothed in bath robes.' A comparatively recent royal wedding would have provided the Welshman with such a wealth of retort that perhaps it is as well for the stratosphere that the discussion preceded the happy event. An altogether English event, with the B.B.C. announcer referring to the son of ' an English King.' And quite rightly, for no one was going to do the English out of this particular opportunity for pageantry of which they are the greatest masters in the world. Even the Society ladies, who wrote exclusive accounts for the press, observed solemnly how the occasion had Lubitsch, the great cinema master, beaten all the way.

Bath robes, then! Why not? The historical fact remains, as Hubert points out, that the Celtic people were the first in the world to invent and use soap, and it is at least a possible conjecture that when the King of a certain invading tribe purloined a cake he was so astonished at the difference it wrought on his person that he instituted the Order of the Bath.

In Scotland we have had Home Rule movements, under many names, over a great number of years. Now there is a Scottish National Party, divorced at last from the Westminster parties, and going all out to achieve for Scotland self-government and the creative power of nationhood. What for? What is it that keeps the Scots seeking in this fashion? What have they lost? What fate are they trying to avert? In the preceding pages I have tried to suggest an answer. In the last resort, if I may be allowed a solitary glint of humour, the Scot cannot remain eternally dumb. Strive as he may at Caledonian gatherings in London to divorce whisky from its proper conjunction with freedom, he succeeds only in making empty if eloquent sounds. He is all dressed up and playing at a tartan game. He is babbling not so much in his own second childhood as in a faraway pantomime childhood of his race. Occasionally, however, some chief in full regalia does break through the ' non-political ' rules to deny and damn Scottish Nationalism with an emphasis that is peculiar.

Personally, I am all for the 1600 wines. If there is anything in the case for our Scottish background, then to deny it full expression is not only to destroy what distinguishes a nation but precisely to that extent to lessen the common spiritual stock of the world.

*   *   *

If whisky has helped me to suggest what lies behind the 'troubles' in the Celtic countries then it has fulfilled a nobler purpose than would any mere historical discussion of itself out of the unused notes, excerpts from Acts of Parliament, literary references, and the other stock-in-trade of the facile book-maker that lie at my elbow—a pretty dry sheaf.

But how can I hope for such apprehension on the part of a reader who may have been drinking beer or tea or, indeed, may be dead sober? I realize now my awful folly; I am visited by the doubt that follows all indulgence in fine spirit, the doubt that has its seat and feet in the stomach. It took the cynical Napoleons of destruction to realize that the armies of humanity march on their bellies.

Even many Nationalists shy clear of anything so unpractical as a spirit. The material things of life are the deciding factors, the ' drift south of industry,' the unemployment, the slums, the classing of one's country as a ' derelict area.' Agreed, with sad cheers. Yet when we see a man beginning to go down at heel and learn his business is going to the devil, we do not form societies to put heels on his boots and charitable money into his affairs, we merely wonder what has happened to *him*, knowing instinctively that if we can get *him* right, the rest will follow.

That seems simple, yet doubtless it is very difficult.

> ' "Let there be licht," said God, and there was
> A little,'

said the Drunk Man as he looked at the Thistle.

*   *   *

Perhaps the literary men do explain something sometimes. Ezra Pound, discussing Wordsworth, observes, ' Artists are the antennæ of the race.' I feel like turning over my literary references after all. And yet—am I to suggest that those who take part annually in the Bacchanalian rite cannot repeat their Burnsian gospel? Absurd! I feel loath as any Englishman—and out of compliment to so charming a neighbour would rather play hunt-the-bottle in his Oxford Dictionary, with its excellent reading and pleasant pastimes, such as: ' Whisky-poker, a harmless non-gambling game, in which the winner gets

a drink and the losers a smell at the cork of the bottle.'
Any ' oration' at such a game would, I feel, at least
have the merit of being spontaneous and terse.

And why quote from the past anyway, as if we
were dealing with a dead subject? The subject is by
no means dead, despite the duty. And now that
Scotland is, so to speak, in the air again, I can see the
spirit quickening everywhere.

Generously, too, like a bottle risen from caves of
the dead. Hugh McDiarmid is not concerned to be
exclusive about whisky, the ' barley bree.' With his
European appetite, he knows there are more drinks
than one capable of moving man to the intense lucidity
of inexplicable utterance.

> ' It matters not what drink is ta'en,
> The barley bree, ambition, love,
> Or Guid or Evil workin' in's,
> Sae lang's we feel like souls set free
> Frae mortal coils and speak in tongues
> We dinna ken and never wull . . .'

The wheels of the universe revolve in as noble and
intricate a measure as the oils in a pure malt whisky
surprised by a drop of water.

Vision! I see Edwin Muir peering like a Druid
into the crystal spirit as it first flows from the still.
There, in what was once a capital, Lewis Spence is
turning a sonnet to the loveliest of all queens, while

in the opposing estuary Blake is putting out from the Tail of the Bank to drum our ghostly vessels down the Clyde. Bridie, the early lover of dry and witty flavours, is now in the middle course of his night holding high wassail in London (a spree that will surprise some Sunday critics before it is over). Linklater can keep his galley in Scotland yet awhile. The Celtic background needs him—to plough it up. And that Pict there, working his earth magic in the den of Kinraddie, and whiles crying his oath of compassion down the vennels of our slums, he is full of the old Pictish marvels and can startle you at the sight of a calf through a whin bush or bring you with an intense hush upon the Grampians in a slap in the dyke. But in this matter, Lewis Grassic Gibbon, compared with McDiarmid, has, as the Irish say, only 'drink taken.' McDiarmid has couped the whole bottle. *A Drunk Man Looks at the Thistle*. I will not pause to enquire whether he affects drunkenness in order (out of a remorseless knowledge of the Presbyterian soul) to give us countenance to look at the nakedness of his awful vision or profoundly believes that the vision may be seen only in that higher state.

> ' Is it the munelicht or a leprosy
>   That spreads aboot me ; and a thistle
>   Or my ain skeleton through wha's bare banes
>   A fiendish wund's begood to whistle ?

The devil's lauchter has a *hwll* like this,
My face has flown open like a lid
—and gibbering on the hillside there
Is a' humanity sae lang has hid! '

Certain it is, that kind of vision was never induced by beer, chianti, sherry, port, or *fine champagne*. It reflects one facet of a Scot's genius—or two facets, the Thistle and Whisky.

Others come crowding upon me, particularly one or two women, but now I begin to perceive with horror my unpardonable guilt—not in using whisky so freely (not at all), but in giving in to the growing public habit of mixing the names of true writers as if they were the ingredients of a damned cocktail (an unfortunate adjective, for a common humanity would save even the damned from cocktails).

Not but that the guilt would be eased if I could refer to any one of them in a few words of power or revelation. I am no poet, however, and can but stare with awe at the ring of light which Henry Vaughan, with God's calm, sets in the heavens :

I saw eternity the other night.

Thought returns to realize it takes a few centuries to distil a line like that.

Vaughan was a Welshman, Vaughan was a Celt. The old jingle takes on a curious irony now. Let it pass.

I am no more than a humble admirer of these

writers of the new spirit, and it merely occurred to me to hope that such as M. Crémieux might not consider my provincial rush to compliment them as too headlong if I say they are a pretty drunken crew, and, in their profound concern for ' the gargoyle at the elbow of the kneeling saint,' not utterly godless.

★   ★   ★

Whereat a certain urge to make a night of it begins to take shape. But I curb it, to save these innocent pages from going up in a lowe.

★   ★   ★

Back to sobriety then and a last word to all those who have known the power and respected the spirit of the national drink. Men of the hills and men of the seas, who when they crossed a friend's threshold were refreshed after their journey or long absence by a glass of the best whisky. I see the cap being removed and hear the Creator being thanked for His mercies and the hostess and host and all the members of the household being blessed both at home and in the lands beyond the seas. It was a speech of the old Gaelic courtesy which the woman of the house accepted with proper grace.

Perhaps this is the vision of the Golden Age that haunts the Scot, and explains much from the warmth of his conviviality to the wild drunken desperation of him at his worst—or best!

PART THREE
WHISKY

WHISKY

WHAT is whisky?

Not even an innocent judge could get an answer to this question, so the Government, harried in the usual way to the proper temperature, offered the witty solution of a Royal Commission. That was in 1908–9, and some of the evidence led was remarkable. The trouble arose in this way. Whisky, the real *uisgebeatha*, had always been distilled from a brew of malted barley (and, in Ireland, of other local grain) by a pot still. I shall presently describe this process in some detail. Round about a hundred years ago, however, there was invented a patent still which managed to extract alcohol from the oddest materials. The product of the pot still contains the oils and aromatic substances that give true whisky its body and flavour. The product of the patent still is almost pure alcohol, flavourless, and is mainly used for industrial and scientific purposes. Methylated spirit is patent still spirit deliberately rendered undrinkable by the addition of unpalatable substances.

Now a patent still produces alcohol much more

cheaply than a pot still and in vastly greater quantities. If, therefore, one can put on the market a bottle of this patent still spirit, reduced with water to the usual retail strength and coloured nicely with caramel, a bigger profit would be obtained from its sale than from the sale of a bottle of pure pot-still whisky. It is the aim of every commercial concern to make as big a profit as possible.

When the Highland and Irish distillers of the real uisgebeatha saw what was happening they became alarmed. This trade of theirs that they had been conscientiously building up for generations was facing disaster, for of course the patent spirit (or ' silent ' spirit as it was called) was being alluringly labelled as fine old matured Scotch whisky. To obtain evidence for the Commission, Revenue officials dropped into 39 public houses in England and 23 in Scotland and asked for ' a glass of whisky.' These drams were taken and officially analysed. All 62 of them were patent still spirit.

The thing had become serious. Moreover the vendors of the silent spirit were growing cunning. ' Whisky is a spirit which owes its flavour to the presence of these curious aromatic substances, and to go and take pure silent spirit and add these aromatic substances which you have made in the laboratory to it, in order to make a fictitious whisky, seems to

me to be going outside the proper bounds of manufacture.' Q. 1824: 'Is that done?' Answer: 'That
is done.' (From Nettleton.)

In fact, one interested blender, before the Commission, defined whisky as 'alcohol mixed with
water.'

Now alcohol can be got from such materials as
sawdust, rotten potatoes, rags, husks, roots, turnips,
oilcake, vegetable waste and refuse, while a gentleman
named Dornig patented a process in 1901 for obtaining
a substitute for ordinary spirit by the dry distillation
of fæces.

According to the press, the Japanese are invading
the foreign market with a liquor they call 'Scotch
Whisky.' The Americans have long shown themselves extraordinarily adept at covering their fire-water
with exact copies of the labels of our more reputable
Scotch blends. What these concoctions may be like,
I do not know, whatever I may guess. But we need
not shudder for ourselves, because in Britain we are
at least saved from having the spirituous products of
these countries palmed off on us as 'Scotch Whisky'
(though it may well occur to us to wonder with
what raw spirit some of our cheaper imported wines
have been fortified abroad). Yet it does seem hard
luck on Scotland that one of her most distinctive
products should be thus imitated throughout the

world. The commercial loss, taking everything that is wrongly labelled 'Scotch' into account, must be enormous; but, as I suggest, surely it is more enormous that so fine and indeed so noble a spirit should be so vilely traduced.

For these and other reasons bearing very directly and importantly on Scotland's welfare, it might be as well if we went with some little care into the manufacture of the true pot-still whisky, followed on with a few facts and reflections on maturing and blending, and even offered some suggestions that might be found useful and profitable to the individual —if a trifle alarming to the wealthier section of the trade.

BARLEY

THE first important thing to learn about our Scottish pot-still whisky is that it is produced entirely from barley. As the best barley gives the largest output and the finest quality, our distillers use the best they can get. If, say, a northern farmer sends a distiller in Speyside a sample of barley that is acceptable but is subsequently found to be above the average in weight and quality of the whole consignment, then there is trouble.

Though formerly all our pot stills were supplied by home farmers, nowadays a considerable quantity of Danish, Danubian, Californian, Australian, and other barleys are imported. These foreign barleys are for the most part dry, light golden in colour from plenty of sun, and of reliable quality. It is difficult to blame a distiller for using them when they can be bought cheaply, and particularly following a season when the home harvest has suffered from rain. No foreign barley, however, beats good home barley either in quality or in quantity of spirit produce, and personally I am persuaded that the home communicates a soft maturing excellence which the foreign barley never has to the same degree. This, I admit, is very difficult to test with certainty, for surely there is no product under the sun that can be so affected in its processes as pot-still whisky or is so sensitive to influences altogether beyond the chemist to isolate and weigh. This may be appreciated as we go along.

With a good stock of dry barley in his grain lofts, the distiller is ready for action. The natural ear of barley, as may be imagined, has to undergo many vicissitudes on its way to the final corked bottle. We need not cumber our own passage with notes on chemico-biological changes. Quite simply, then, the distiller's aim is, first, to ensure that the large mass of starch, held together by proportionately small quantities of albuminous matter, of which all grain is composed, is changed from an insoluble to a soluble condition; second, that this soluble starch is converted into sugar in order that it be fermented or turned into alcohol; and, third, that the alcoholic wash so formed be boiled off into whisky: these three divisions of his labour he calls respectively, malting, brewing, and distilling.

MALTING

FROM the grain loft, the barley is removed to a cistern where it is steeped in water for a period varying from two to three days according to the time of year, the kind of barley, and the weather conditions (typical uncertain quantities!). From the steep the barley is spread out on a stone floor to a depth of two to three feet. The water-sodden grains soon begin to germinate and the head maltman is very careful about the rising temperature (which sets in with germination), the appearance of the first rootlet, and the surrounding atmospheric conditions. If this bed of growing barley were left undisturbed, the five rootlets which follow their leader in each ear would soon become entangled with the myriads of other rootlets and a hopeless matted mess would result. The grain is therefore turned over expertly and periodically with wooden shovels and the bed or couch gradually thinned out until at the end of from eight to twelve days it is only some three to four inches deep. By this time the acrospire or growing stem has almost reached the point of coming through the husk and the starch has

become soft and chalky. As one old maltman put it :
' When you can write your name on the wall with it
(the ear), it's ready.'

The growth must now be stopped, though the
withering of the rootlets has already set in on the
great stone floors where the maltmen have continued
at regular intervals to scatter the grain in showers
with rhythmical sweeps of their wooden shovels—
an attractive sight to watch, and one that has always
been to me, for some obscure reason, a little foreign,
as though it belonged more rightly to the great barns
of the granaries of a Europe still with the rhythm in
its labour of the mediæval age. But, despite all the
Gaelic labour tunes behind them, these maltmen do
not sing at their work—possibly for the same reason
as prompts the reader to smile at the thought of it
in this commercial age.

From the wide floors with their many pillars, the
grain is now removed to the kiln (with its pagoda-like
cowl) to be thoroughly dried over a peat fire—helped
out when required with coke. This is a very important operation and one that must be proceeded
with carefully, or irreparable damage will be done.
The aim is to start with a low temperature and
gradually to increase it as the grain dries until there
are finally produced ears of barley that are crisp,
tasty, easily ground, and aromatic, and henceforth to

be called *malt*. To get even drying, the grain has been regularly turned on the wire plates of the kiln through which the peat smoke has been continuously ascending. The last kiln I was in had an electric globe that glimmered high up in the dense gloom like a ghostly star while the maltman, with bent shoulders, shuffled up and down, up and down, like a figure in some inferno.

I have referred to things beyond the chemist's power to detect, and perhaps here in a single instance I might make my meaning clear if I indicated the effect of this peat smoke on the flavour of the whisky. Though the smoke does no more than rise through the grain while it is being dried on the kiln, it yet contrives to impart a peaty fragrance which persists throughout all the processes of fermentation and distillation, and can be distinctly detected in the spirit after it has been lying in a cask for twenty years; in fact it constitutes one of the flavours that a perfect whisky should possess.

In all this malting process, skilled judgment is needed, for the goodness of the malt determines not only the quantity of alcohol that may result from its fermentation but the quality of the ultimate distillate itself.

BREWING

THE malt is now cleansed of the rootlets ('combings') and any other impurities, and in due course is sent along to be crushed in the mill-room.

With the crushed malt in its hopper and hot water in the boiling copper, we are ready for the next stage called *mashing*. The hot water and the crushed malt meet and fall together into a great round vessel called the mash tun, where they lie for some two hours in a communion that gives birth to a very important issue. As has been said, the object of malting was to break up and render more or less soluble the starch and albumen in the barley grains. This has now been done and the soluble albuminous body (called diastase) in the mash tun, with the water at a suitable temperature (145° to 155° F.), begins to act upon the starch and to convert it into sugar (maltose) and dextrin. As much maltose as possible is desired and as little dextrin (which may be regarded as intermediate between starch and sugar). This conversion of the starch to sugar is absolutely essential.

The change that takes place in the mash tun is quite noticeable. From a cloudy insipid gruel the liquid becomes semi-transparent and sweet. It is then drawn off and on its way to the vessel where it is to be fermented it is rapidly cooled to round about 70° F. What is left in the mash tun is again mixed with hot water and the solution drawn off, for it is the business of the brewer to dissolve out the whole of the saccharine matter.

The grain husks and other residue left in the mash tun make good cattle-feeding and the farmers of the neighbourhood come and cart it away—at a price. Distilling in the Highlands is usually carried on between October and May. It is suspended during the summer months for various reasons: difficulties of water supply, malting, cooling, etc.—including this rather important commercial one of getting an easy and immediate market for the waste grains (draff), as cattle, of course, do not require artificial feeding at this season. Distilling thus works into the economy of the Highlands in a very natural way, and even this ‘silent season’ at the distillery itself is required for overhauling plant, securing fresh supplies of barley and peat, erecting and gauging vessels, tidying up warehouses, and otherwise preparing for the next working season. I am tempted to expatiate on this absolute naturalness of the industry to its Highland environment. It is a true growth, whereby tradition, ways of life and labour, climate and soil, flower into an art that could never be achieved so perfectly elsewhere.

But meantime we have left some ten thousand gallons of saccharine solution—wort—in a round wooden vessel called a wash back. The sugar in this wort has now got to be turned into alcohol, and to help towards this end a few buckets of yeast are added in order as quickly as possible to set the whole in a ferment.

Yeast, for all its extraordinary capacity to set things seething, is really a delicate plant of a rather low order whose minute cells grow by a process of budding, yet in prime condition amidst prime wort it causes the liveliest commotion that I know of in nature. It needs oxygen to breathe, and as the oxygen of the air is kept away from it in the wash back, it turns upon the sugar to take the oxygen out of that, and in the process decomposes it into alcohol and carbonic acid. That anyway and roughly is Pasteur's theory of what takes place. A very old *Handbook for Young Brewers* puts it another way: 'Pasteur holds that the living organisms of the yeast-plant absorb a large quantity of the saccharin liquid (in addition to albuminous matter and dextrin consumed), a small portion of which it eats up, as it were, excreting the remainder as carbonic acid and alcohol.'

There are other theories, but it may be taken as proved that the yeast-plant is a doughty fellow for all that he is of a low order and therefore given to gluttony, eructations, and other Rabelaisian amusements.

He goes to work innocently enough in that huge vessel by sending up bubbles that plop softly, but very soon a seething is heard and the wort appears to be actually thinking of boiling. A frothy head forms and slowly rises up through the three feet or so that separate the surface of the liquid from the top of the vessel. It would, of course, come right over the top if the brewer did not switch it back. Nowadays wooden switchers are rotated by mechanism, but I have seen men in past days, stripped to the waist, with long birch sticks laying into the ebullient yeast-froth for dear life in a battle in which they were not always completely victorious. With the automatic switchers going full speed, I have heard one of these backs rock and roar in a perfect reproduction of a really dirty night at sea.

Let me explain that the specific gravity of the original wort is about 1050° (water = 1000), and that in the process of fermentation the gravity gradually decreases to about 998°. In practical language, it goes down through (attenuates) some 50°, attaining its maximum commotion in the middle period.

One night in the tun-room a large back was having a fearsome battle with the switchers. The old brewer, a close friend of mine, was growing anxious, for the vessel was swaying on her bottom, with sides heaving.

'Is she at her worst?' I cried.

'Not yet.'

'At what degree will she be at her worst?'

'At twenty-one, like a woman,' he answered.

When things have quietened down a bit, it is a trick of some of the tun-room men to slide back a section of the wooden lid and ask a visitor to sniff the aroma. As the gas is carbonic acid, the effect on nostrils and lungs is as sharp as an electric shock on the fingers and much more unpleasant.

With the fierce life declining, the head falls back and in due course there supervenes a state of spent quietude. A short life and a rousing one! But not an end. For this body has been no more than preparing itself to be turned into true spirit. It might please Rabelais to reflect that the more rousing the life, the surer is the brewer of a generous quantity of spirit. Not but that a slower, gentler fermentation may produce a more saintly spirit. There is always an ideal in those things. But where so much can go wrong, the brewer is always happy to see a merry ferment.

There are the experts, of course, who say that distillery ferments are frequently too rapid; and certainly when the temperature of the wash rises much beyond 92° or 93° the spirit to be distilled from it is going to be badly affected. In high temperatures are largely created the coarse alcohols and acids and pungent aldehydes which catch a man's nose and throat when he takes a glass of the finished whisky years afterwards. This but instances once more the great care that has to be exercised at every point in the elaborate process of making fine whisky. The frequent presence of the unforeseen and incalculable raises distilling from what we commonly understand as a manufacture to a true art.

Though, to return to my point, you will get wash that will throw a very small head yet ferment and snivel away with an ominous fieriness, while wash that takes the switchers like a sea may develop no more than a healthy temperature.

In fact, with every care exercised, things can go more mysteriously and disastrously wrong in the wash back than anywhere else. Every degree of the 50 that the 10,000 gallons of wort (or wash as it is called when fermentation has started) attenuates is equal to slightly over 20 gallons of proof spirit. If, therefore, instead of coming down to 998°, the wash sticks finally at, say, 1003°, the loss in that one vessel is

equal to about two hogsheads of proof spirit. This
happens now and then for reasons which no one
can certainly explain. Bad yeast, uncleanliness, impurities in the mashing water, or other excuse may
be offered. But only the brewer knows with what
trepidation he starts on his next week's work.

DISTILLING

FERMENTATION having been completed, the wash is now ready for distillation. In the still-house, there are at least two stills: a Wash Still and a Low Wines Still. In shape they are pretty much what they must have been in early times (the sort of romantic shape that artist-illustrators use when depicting the alchemist in his den): the round copper pot narrowing into a tall neck which bends over and downwards as it penetrates the wall of the still-house. Outside, this neck is continued as a pipe which doubles and redoubles on itself at great length (the ‘worm’) in a tank of circulating cold water, whence it finally emerges to enter the receiver-room where there are vessels all ready to receive what it offers. In the normal Highland distillery the content of the wash still may be anything from 2000 to 4000 gallons. When this still receives its proper charge of wash, the furnace underneath is set going and the stillman stands by.

The stillman's job is one of great responsibility, for negligence on his part may not only wreck the still, but, what can hardly be detected at the time, ruin the flavour of the final spirit. Considering his comparatively small wage, his faithfulness to his task is surely a tribute to the Highland worker. Indeed it may be said here that distillery workers as a class of men are amongst the most trustworthy and obliging and pleasantly mannered in these Islands. I have seen amusing evidences of rivalry between men of different stills when they forgather on a Saturday night and make comparisons of the weekly produce (i.e. of the quantity of spirit to the centesimal point produced from each bushel of malt). Not that much of the truth is given away where the week has been an indifferent one! Though bitterness can creep in too. A very human little community, whose material welfare, one hopes, may become much higher as responsibility, not merely to employers, but in a greater sense to the community of the nation and to that nation's good name in other lands, is more generally realized. To be the makers of something that is the finest of its kind in the world should inspire a good wage as well as a feeling of honour and trust.

Meantime the temperature of the wash is rising and the stillman, by tapping the neck of the still with a slung wooden ball, is able to detect exactly what is going on inside. If the wash were allowed to boil merrily it would boil over, like a pan of milk, and coming rushing in through the worm to the receiver-room, would foul all the vessels and even flood the floor. But by skilled attention to the furnace and its draughts the stillman persuades the still to behave quietly and decently so that vapour only rises up and passes into the worm there to be condensed, and make its first appearance in a gentle trickle into the safe, which is a box with glass sides and certain sampling instruments, fixed between the end of the incoming pipe and the collecting vessel.

Soon the trickle has become a steady flow and the stillman can relax his anxiety. Seven to eight hours should see the charge worked off, that is, all the spirit withdrawn from the wash, leaving behind in the still some 70 per cent. of the original quantity as ' spent wash,' which is normally run down the sewer. Here let it be explained that the boiling point of ethyl alcohol (*the* alcohol) is 173° F., while that of water is 212° F. But wash contains all sorts of secondary constituents, such as higher alcohols, acids, ethers, aldehydes, and so on (in minute degree, of course) whose various boiling points for the most part are higher than that of water. By running his still slowly, and in particular seeing that his fire is dying down as his testing instrument in the safe shows the distillate to be nearing water, he can prevent to some extent

the passing over of objectionable substances, leaving
them wisely to go down the drain.

This first distillate of the wash is called ' low wines.'
It is weak, impure spirit, offensive to the nostrils, and
quite undrinkable. It is pumped into the second or
low wines still there to be redistilled.

The first flow from the worm of this second still
is what is popularly known as ' foreshot.' It is the
strongest spirit that the still delivers but is highly
contaminated with oil which it holds in solution.
Water mixed with this strong spirit turns it cloudy
in the sampling glass in the safe. Very carefully the
stillman keeps testing the new run until, reduced
with water to some 30° under proof, the spirit remains
quite clear in his glass. Now at last he has got the
real whisky and promptly switches the flow into the
spirit receiver, where whisky and whisky only is
collected—in due course to be pumped to an outside
store and there filled into casks.

Not that the whisky is now freed entirely from
oils, as the naked eye may confirm when water has
been added to it; some essential principle is retained
that gives pot-still whisky its peculiar, desirable, and
unmistakable flavour.

As distillation goes on the spirit steadily weakens
in strength, and again the stillman, with his sampling
tubes and glass hydrometers, tests it carefully, for as

in the beginning so towards the end, added water turns it cloudy. What is not collected in the spirit receiver is called ' feints ' which is distilled again in the same still along with the low wines from the wash still. In this way the circuit is kept going and the stillman busy. And as I have said already, his responsibility is grave, for he has only to run some of the impure product for a short time into the spirit receiver to give the whole a pungent, feinty, objectionable flavour, more readily detected by the palate ten years afterwards than there and then in the crystal distillate.

When his hydrometer gives the reading of ' water ' the stillman knows that the charge in his still is exhausted and accordingly he prepares to run the residue —the ' spent lees '—down the sewer.

The whole process of brewing and distilling occupies one week (Monday to Saturday), the first part of the week being devoted to brewing and the second to continuous distilling.

All this work takes place under regular supervision of an Excise official whose business it is to see that no spirit goes illicitly into consumption. With duty at £3, 12s. 6d. a proof gallon this is naturally important, especially when a few thousand gallons are made at a distillery each week. Long experience has created an almost perfect system of supervision, interfering so little with practical operations and supplying such figures of liability or accountancy as distillers un-hesitatingly accept, that normally the relations between the Excise official and the distiller are pleasant and charged with mutual respect. The disgruntled dis-tiller and pompous official are still to be met, though with sufficient rarity to provide little more than an occasional good joke.

I am only too well aware that the foregoing is a very rough and ready summary of the way in which fine whisky is produced at a pot still. But if I have been able to suggest the great care that has to be exercised at every point in the elaborate process and the naturalness with which it finds a tradition and home in the Highland environment, I should feel satisfied.

MATURING

THE whisky collected in the spirit receiver is in strength round about 15 to 20 over proof. (Patent still spirit is 66 to 69 over proof; pure alcohol is 73.) It might be as well here to try to explain what proof spirit means. 'Proof' officially means the strength of proof as ascertained by Sykes's hydrometer. It is purely an arbitrary standard and expressed in words denotes a spirit which at the temperature of 51° F. weighs 12/13 of an equal measure of distilled water. More simply, if you take equal weights of pure alcohol and water and mix them you have proof spirit. If you want to reduce a hundred gallons of proof spirit to 30 under proof, you add roughly 42 gallons of water. Retail whisky is 30 under proof. For pot-still whisky this in my opinion is too weak a strength. Many fine Highland whiskies develop a slight cloudiness when over-diluted with water. The pre-war strength of 20 under proof is to be desired; and if still a shade stronger, all the better; for then when water is added before drinking certain etheric aromas are freshly liberated and there is awakened a subtle life which is missed in the deadness of weak spirit which has been standing some time. However, we had perhaps better come at this matter of what is desirable more methodically.

When the spirit has been removed to the filling store, it is reduced to about 11 over proof in the vat before being drawn off into cask. This strength is considered by Scottish distillers as the ideal one for maturing purposes.

Of course at this stage the spirit (being a distillate) is crystal clear, and would so remain indefinitely unless deliberately coloured. In taste it is not unpleasant though very penetrating to the delicate membranes of the mouth. To sniff the vat immediately after it has been emptied is to get a keen rather exquisite fragrance, but so much one of pure essence that it is elusively difficult to name. A few drops of this potent liquid would burn its way down an unaccustomed throat to the accompaniment of gasping and tears. Yet I knew distillery workmen who could toss off half-a-tumblerful without facial distortion or audible exhalation of any kind, and always without the slightest noticeable effect on physical control. Humanly and decently, too: 'It's a better morning . . . but it looks as if it might come to rain again.' (Here dots really represent a short potent interval!) For at one time the dramming of distillery workmen, night and morning, with this white spirit, duty free, was allowed by the Excise authorities. But, of course, the Powers of Temperance grew jealous of such trafficking with the Powers of Darkness, and so the men lost their right to the dram they made. I have heard a few sad stories of hard-working men of eighty odd winters who were so disheartened by the official edict of abstinence that they gave up their distillery jobs and shortly afterwards died.

But it is time we returned to the full casks now being rolled into warehouse, there in years of semi-darkness to undergo the mysterious process of maturation.

Who first discovered that whisky improved by being kept in wood, no one seems to know. Most great discoveries have been accidental, however, and it is at least very probable that some smuggler's keg was once upon a time hidden in a hurry and through some simple mischance to its owner—such as violent death—not brought to light again for many years. The discoverer—Discoverer II—would have convened an extraordinary meeting of the communal brotherhood. Possibly there is here a lost fascinating history of how whole moors were specially dug up to hide and mature whisky kegs, much as houses were once burned down in China to provide roast pig!

The real history of the Highlands has never yet

been written. When Mr John Buchan in the first page of his *Montrose* refers to the Highland line separating for centuries 'some semblance of civilization [in Lowlands] from its stark opposite' he was indulging in a fiction which Mr Evan Barron characterizes as 'monstrous.' It is difficult not to admire the nice precision of that adjective. Continuous clan feuds to the accompaniment of dark barbarities form the romantic staple of historians and novelists when dealing with Highland people. The other day I was reading some charter-chest records of a great western clan during the 'stark opposite' period—to find that three successive generations of clansmen knew nothing of fighting on even a local scale! If Mr Buchan could equal this in the last century of English or European civilization one should perhaps be able to appreciate more readily his indulgence in verbal barbarities.

Chemists are unable to state what precisely takes place during maturation in the wood. The palate, however, knows quite well. During the first year or two, whisky (to my palate at least) goes dead off. I should far rather have it direct from the spirit vat while it still has the fresh aromatic cleanness of a new creation. In these early years of maturing it becomes gawky and angular, an early green adolescence capable of being very self-conscious and horrid between the first marvel of birth and the final round fulness of maturity.

That whisky may not be sold until it is three years old is a sound law—that would be all the sounder if the minimum age was raised to five, as in the Irish Free State and Australia. (Not that this matters so much in the case of patent-still spirit where maturation is negligible however long it is kept.) At seven to eight years a pot-still whisky may be fully matured in a small cask. In a sound hogshead (55 gallons) ten years are sufficient. The finest whisky I have ever tasted came out of a butt (110 gallons) that had been maturing undisturbed on the ground floor of a ware-house for fifteen years. This whisky, I admit, was very insidious. One could not quite credit its ex-cellence. Try it as one liked—and when one liked—it was still excellent. Possibly the true Calvinistic soul, a little disappointed, a little revulsed, by such earthly perfection, desired to find the imperfection, instinctively needed it to ensure the continuance of this Scottish scheme of things entire. Is not perfection on this earth rank heresy? The heresy was hunted as assiduously as our forebears hunted the witch. But where they condemned and burned we, so much less fortunate, could neither condemn nor burn (even the slight internal heat that *was* generated was dis-appointingly pleasant). It was very sad, though a wry amusment could sometimes be extracted from watching surprise light a stranger's eye. Sensuously, spiritually, metaphysically, and scientifically—it was tried in that order yet evaded conviction. One man, given to the new interpretation of Scottish history (a suspected Nationalist) advanced the revolutionary suggestion that we should simply accept it as perfect, but immediately one of the old school, sensing some subtle affront to England or the Empire, said he would sooner drink the whole cask. The owner of the cask smiled. It was a very difficult situation—that solved itself in perhaps characteristic national fashion. It was the springtime of the year when other things than the fancies of young men and the breasts of little birds are affected. To listen to the silence of 5000 casks of whisky in the twilight of a warehouse while the barley seed is being scattered on surrounding fields, might make even a Poet Laureate dumb. To be a fifteen-year-old butt waiting in a cellar to be removed for bottling, public exhibition, and the foul language of the soda syphon, is perhaps to know the ultimate note in individual tragedy. Anyway, the end hoops of that cask burst one spring night, and in the morning the owner could hold all that was left in a wine glass.

After fifteen years in wood, whisky as a rule begins to deteriorate. The size of the cask is important, of course. In a nine-gallon cask the number of square inches of internal surface exposed to a bulk gallon is 106; in a hogshead it is 60; and in a butt, 48. The smaller the cask the greater is the percentage of loss through absorption, transfusion, exposure to damp or cold or heat, and therefore the quicker does the whisky in it mature—and deteriorate. For as whisky matures in wood it slowly goes down both in strength and bulk. At fifteen years a quarter cask would be faintly woody in flavour. I once tasted whisky out of a hogshead, eighteen years old. During that time it had diminished in strength from 11 over proof to 10 under proof and in bulk by about ten gallons. It was incredibly mild and smooth, and could be sipped neat as a liqueur. Well-bred, perfectly mannered, without a gesture, it would never burst its hoops except by accident. It had really attained philosophic quietude. But when a few drops of water were added, there came to the palate a faint woodiness, very elusive, but there, like a thought of dissolution. Keats, haunted by death, might have pinned a sonnet to its bung-cloth. Which is enough to make one think of the cask itself smiling in Speyside kindliness to that pale face: 'Tak' a wee drop, laddie. God kens ye need it.'

I wonder if it would be safe to say that the most desirable flavours in whisky are produced on the malt-kiln and in the cask; the worst in the brewing and distilling? Probably not, yet there certainly is a working truth in the remark. Anyhow, the kind of cask and its position in the warehouse are two very important factors in the production of a fine finished whisky.

Casks are made of oak wood (other woods—I have known chestnut—are to be absolutely avoided) and may be divided into three kinds: plain, treated, and sherry.

The sherry cask is the most expensive and most sought after. Whisky, it will be remembered, is originally crystal clear. How does it acquire its golden or ruddy colour? Generally from the wood of the cask. It is remarkable that an absolutely empty butt, because it once contained sherry, will colour over one hundred gallons of clear spirit during the process of maturing. The spirit draws out the wine that had soaked into the wood and diffuses it throughout its bulk. And, still more remarkable, years afterwards, when the cask is emptied and filled again it will once more colour the hundred odd gallons, though now very palely. This is known as a second-fill cask.

A perfectly plain cask will not of course colour the spirit in any way, and in a certain public-house in Inverness, as I write this, Glen Grant whisky (one of the finest) may be had in this clear state.

A treated cask is a plain cask which has been internally dosed with a certain vinous compound in order that the spirit may be coloured as in a sherry cask. This ' blending wine ' is sometimes claimed in advertisement to impart a three years' mellowness to the new spirit and even to add a certain body or fulness. The advertised claim is not only wrong but unfortunate, for one does not think of body or palate fulness in whisky in the same way as one does in port, while none of all the various methods for artificially maturing whisky, from aeration to electrocution (America is fecund in producing ageing systems), is of any use. All that colouring does whether indirectly from the treated wood or directly by the brutal addition of a caramel solution, is to mask the natural directness of young whisky and thus appear to give it a smoothness which to the experienced palate is not only fictitious but mawkish and, when overdone, slightly slimy, like the thought of something drowned in a ditch. The true sherry colour gives the spirit a golden glow right to its living core, and may be detected by the naked eye when placed against the ruddy dulness of a ' treated ' spirit.

Something of this unnatural fulness may be got even from a sherry cask which had originally contained a rich variety of ' dark brown.' The bouquet from such a cask, eight or nine years old, is that of sherry etherealized and is extremely pleasant. But the taste can be just a trifle too smooth, too full, too fleshly, to a palate concerned rather with the spirit. Personally I prefer whisky from a sherry wood that leaves it pale as amber, light as straw, with something for the palate that is no more than a vague memory of those sunny Mediterranean countries that continue to haunt our northern pre-Celtic minds. As for the matured crystal spirit—well, I am doing my best to be severely practical and to avoid the higher meta-physics.

Wood can vary from good to bad, whether sherry or plain. A damp warehouse diminishes the strength of the spirit but keeps up its bulk, while a dry ware-house does exactly the reverse. The former type of storage is the better for maturing, though then one must be on guard against the growth of moulds that may penetrate defective wood and impart a musty flavour after many years. Mustiness may be acquired in other ways: by the original use of damp or mouldy grain or malt, impure water, bad yeast, or generally from vessels not thoroughly cleansed. As we have already seen, woodiness comes from excessive age in cask; and some of the coarse rank flavours—so disastrous to a single whisky, however suitable for blending—are defects from brewing and distilling, occasionally in the case of wild fermentation heats very difficult to foresee, but in the case of distilling largely a matter of lack of sufficient care by the stillman.

I have so far refrained from making direct reference to the nature of the water used in the various operations at a distillery. It is popularly supposed that the water of our Highland burns is an absolute essential and thus explains why the true malt whisky can be made only in the Highlands. A chemist is not impressed by this belief, I understand. All he knows is that the water used for steeping the grain, mashing the malt, and reducing the spirit should be pure, and that the water from our Highland burns can no doubt be got in a pretty pure state. He is right—as far as he goes. But in this matter he is always subject to the palate—and the sensitive palate detects flavours that baffle the chemist to measure or weigh, as, for example, the existence of the peat aroma twenty years after. All we are certain of is that uncontaminated water from a Highland burn has proved the best water for making pot-still whisky. A big firm of blenders in London actually advertise that the water they use for reducing purposes is taken from north of the Grampians by train in large porcelain tanks. And particularly important is the water used for reducing the spirit in the distillery store before filling into cask, for whether hard or soft water is there used, can sometimes be detected by the naked eye and certainly is an influence for bad or good respectively in subsequent maturation.

Briefly, then, the maturing of whisky is a natural slow process, during which an ethereal aroma is developed and the pungent taste of the new spirit gradually disappears giving place to a mellowness and flavour that suggest body without loss of cleanness to the taste. To produce this highly desirable result in its most perfect state has required close attention at every stage of an intricate and finally long process : sound matured barley (to be initially kiln-dried if showing the slightest trace of damp), pure water in the steep, correct germination, even and thorough kiln-drying of the malt (very important), proper mashing and fermentation heats, avoidance of infection of wort and wash from the air, the use of healthy yeast, the cleanliness of all vessels and particularly the systematic and thorough cleansing of all wash backs, regulated heats in the stills, the prevention of frothing and fouling by a stillman jealous of his skill, the selection of sound well-hooped casks, the conditions of storage—whether damp or dry, cold, hot, or draughty, and the examination once a week of each one of the thousands of casks during its allotted span of years in these vast duty-free distiller's warehouses.

No wonder the quality of pot-still whisky varies;

no wonder chemists and others can deal more positively with patent-still spirit that as practically pure alcohol offers few difficulties or complexities in manufacture or in maturation; and perhaps it is no wonder that blenders, for their greater profit, got an indiscriminating public to prefer a tasteless alcohol that masks its kick under a touch of pretty colour.

*   *   *

After writing these words, I had rather a remarkable experience in Edinburgh where my host, a Caithness man, produced a bottle of whisky whose contents were beyond any shadow of doubt over 104 years old. The cork was thickly waxed, and the side of the bottle bore a heavy seal with ' SCRABSTER 1830 ' stamped clearly in circular form. I thought this seal was also of wax, but on trying it with my knife discovered that it was actually embossed in the glass of the bottle. (So that presumably the bottle was home-made as well as the contents.) The glass was smoke-dark in colour and the bottle stood the least trifle awry, gaining thereby somewhat in individuality without loss of dignity. This bottle had been presented to my friend by his mother, to whom it had been given as a wedding gift in 1880.

Whisky is generally believed to mature in wood but not in bottle. Assuming this liquor was bottled immediately after it was made—and the 1830 on the glass would rather imply as much—then here was an occasion for the perfect experiment!

Let it be said at once that the liquor in that bottle was matured to an incredible smoothness. I have never tasted anything quite like it in that respect, yet it had an attractively objectionable flavour, somewhere between rum and tar, to our palates. I suggested that the malt must have been dried over a peat fire into which some ship timber—probably gathered on the Pentland shore—had been introduced. But my host hit on what undoubtedly had happened. In these old days, when it was the custom to have a fire on the middle of the floor with a hole in the roof for chimney, some specks of the old glistening soot from the rafters had fallen amongst the malt. Perhaps during the first few years of maturation this might hardly have been detected—or, again, may have been deliberately aimed at as an elusive part of the whole flavour!—but certainly in this extreme age it was all-pervasive; it had become, indeed, the spirit's very breath.

I do not wish to imply that we made martyrs of ourselves, like the first Discoverer, but the experiment required, amongst other things, considerable talk, during the course of which my host produced a much older heirloom in the shape of a linen tablecloth that had been woven by a lady on her own loom in that same northern district of Caithness from flax grown around her own door. Into one corner of the cloth she had worked her initials in her own golden hair—still as bright in colour as the bridal dream that must so often have glistened behind her young eyes. Lovely eyes; lovely enough, we gravely decided before the evening was over, to make even an anti-Highland historian blush!

BLENDING

I was talking to-day to an old Highland distiller who recounted with great amusement the story of the two monkeys. As evidence for the Commission in its task of deciding 'What is Whisky?' two monkeys were treated, he told me, one with patent-still spirit and the other with pot-still whisky. The patent or 'silent' monkey developed in his cups a vicious temper, spitting and snarling like a tinker far gone in meth., while his fellow, mellowed with all malt, grew drunkenly benign. When they became sober, the test was reversed, and now the monkey that had been vicious staggered about in the utmost good nature, while his fellow, breathing the silent spirit, cursed like a trooper.

I did not suggest that the experiment warranted legal interference on the plea of cruelty to animals, for I could not know what the monkeys thought. I do know, however, of a publican in a northern town whose son, a seaman, had brought him home a monkey. Being as intelligent as most of his kind, this monkey learned in due course to turn on and off the tap of a two-gallon whisky jar and so help himself to a small one neat. One day, however, in aberrant excitement, he forgot to turn off the tap and his master entered to find the jar empty and the better part of two gallons of excellent liquor on the floor. There was a scene and a staggeringly rapid exit on the part of the monkey. The poor brute complained bitterly, if somewhat inarticulately, to the neighbours, but his master, against all subsequent persuasion, remained adamantly irreconcilable. What finally happened to the monkey I do not know. The master was one day found dead in a ditch on his way home from a fair.

A patent still is an affair of two tall columns, heated by steam, into which wash is poured at one end and out of which practically pure alcohol pours at the other. For industrial and scientific purposes it is an invention of very great and ever-increasing value. In this country, ten years ago the materials used were malt and unmalted grain (mostly maize) with smaller quantities of rice and molasses. Now the quantity of malt used is small and that of molasses some four times greater than all other materials put together.

By the Finance Act of 1933, however, 'spirits described as Scotch Whisky shall not be deemed to correspond to that description unless they have been obtained by distillation in Scotland from a mash of cereal grains saccharified by the diastase of malt and have matured in a bonded warehouse for a period of at least three years.'

This does not help pot-still whisky much, as the product of a patent still in Scotland using (let us say by way of illustration) 10 per cent. malt and 90 per cent. maize qualifies for the right to the designation Scotch Whisky. All it really boils down to is that industrial spirits made in England shall not now be described *on official documents* as Scotch Whisky. It has definitely helped the patent still in Scotland that distils from a cereal mash (largely maize).

The great blending industry in Scotland arose with the patent still, and at the present time our most famous blends are mixtures of pot and patent still spirits in proportions which we do not know, but in which the preponderance is believed to be heavily patent. If you take a vat of 1000 gallons of patent spirit and add 100 gallons of pot-still whisky, any chemical analyst can truthfully say that the result contains all the natural properties of a pot-still whisky. And in that respect there is no law about what the blender may put on his label. Yet the blender could very easily tell us what surely we have a right to know by stating on his label the proportions of patent and pot still and their respective ages. Nothing could be simpler. All reputable wines carry their vineyard and their year. A fine pot-still whisky is as noble a product of Scotland as any burgundy or champagne is of France. Patent-still spirit is no more a true whisky than, at the opposite extreme, is any of those cheap juices of the grape heavily fortified by raw spirit which we import from the ends of the earth a true wine. One can imagine M. Crémieux sniffing one of these inky fluids—as he would sniff a flower!

And not only is the true product of our Highland glens misrepresented or damned on the market, but is murderously discriminated against by the Government. Colonial wine containing up to 42° of alcohol pays a duty of 4s. a gallon. If it were taxed on the same basis (alcoholic content) as whisky (70°) the duty would be over 30s. a gallon! In the poor quarters of our industrial towns in Scotland a thriving trade is now being carried on in these heavy wines, for a man can buy a glass of the stuff, complete with kick, for fourpence. If he carries it away and adds a dash of methylated spirits, he can get roaring fou' on sixpence—and have the satisfaction that he is encouraging international trade and brotherhood: methylated spirits from England out of the molasses of the West Indies, heavy wines from Australia or Spain, and the discriminating palate from Scotland—that country whose history has shown that her children have always been concerned with the things of the

spirit. I am tempted to wonder what the fervid anti-
nationalist would make of this hectic effort at a
spirituous world-state. It would be really a trifle
difficult for him to explain it away, for surely no
trade is so perfectly organized as the liquor trade.
Intelligence, cash, international contacts and outlook—
everything except actual legislative power. Would
he give them that also?

This is something worth thinking over, for it does
suggest a basic weakness in the big-business internationalism of our popular, if sentimental, thinkers.
Those who aspire towards the brotherhood of man
so frequently show a spirit not too brotherly. Mr
Clissold, for whom I have an irrational affection,
refers, for example, to the Russian experiment in
brotherhood as ' a project-shaped vacuum,' ' the sabot-
age of civilization,' inspired by a foreign gentleman,
studying in the British Museum, who was ' imperfectly
aerated ' and ' a maggot.' Who can help abrupt
laughter at the marvellous self-assurance of this
English mind! Not that the epithets were blatantly
applied, of course, because Mr Clissold believes that
the world-state of his scientific dream is a revolutionary
conception to be realized by an intelligent minority
who, instead of using violence, will merely emanate
' an intimation of superior strength.' Really charming
fellows.

Yet how can an ordinary man help being impressed by the ' maggots ' who believe and act, not in words at the ends of the earth, but with deeds in their own land, in their own homes? They are trying to metamorphose themselves first. And that seems to have been the basis of all true morality and, in its personal effort, of philosophy and science, since the world began.

If only we had some of that zeal in Scotland in this matter of whisky! Indeed this matter of whisky is so appropriate a symbol of our general condition that it keeps me digressing in this unfortunate manner. We have the most perfect whisky in the world. What are we doing about it? Hauling down the red lion on its golden field and hoisting in place thereof Red Biddy on a field sable. Out of the ancient things of the spirit we have created a Spectre of the Shawl, complete with emaciated flesh and talons, forever wandering, our *belle dame sans merci*, in the tenebrous vennels of our industrial lands. A trifle overdrawn, perhaps? Perhaps; and possibly a trifle underdrawn. We were always the deuce of a people for nice distinctions.

To come back to the blends, for justice shall be done until the pot stills collapse. In a certain exclusive Highland club where blends rule, a self-whisky out of one of our finest pots was introduced once upon a time, I am told—and duly dismissed by a conjoint palate that discovered it (the whisky) had a taste.

There, then, is the blender's excuse or reason: he has to give the public what it wants. And he does it perfectly, devoting great skill and care to the business—far greater skill and care, to pay him a due compliment, than the need warrants. For when pretence is removed, what is really desired is a taste-less alcohol. An industrial spirit, out of molasses or sawdust, detained for three years in a sherry cask, reduced to 30 under proof, poured into a glass and frothed up with soda water, makes as smooth a drink as the heart of a clubman desires. After polo or corporation golf, it refreshingly hits the spot. Whisky is now being dashed with lemonade and added to a glass of cider. So long as the 'whisky' is pure patent spirit, a man is correctly fortifying his lemonade —which possibly needs it—and cider. But in the case of a fine matured pot-still whisky . . . I have never tried a delicate wine of the Loire stiffened with stout nor yet a *fine champagne* laced with liquorice, so possibly I am only letting prejudice blow its bubbles.

Your clubman, then, desires a blend, something which he feels is 'light' and easily taken, and your blender supplies it. Accordingly the blender has become the dictator of the pot still, whose product he uses. To survive, the pot still must sell to him as cheaply as possible and must therefore contrive to get the maximum amount of spirit out of the minimum amount of barley. Nor is that all, for if the pot-still product is too fine, too delicate, in other words if it is a highly desirable single whisky, it will not communicate in sufficient measure to a waiting vat of patent spirit the characteristics of a Highland malt whisky; but, on the other hand, if it contains these characteristics in excessive degree, making it pungent and rather objectionable as a single whisky, it then achieves perfection for blending, on the principle that a little of it goes a long way.

That is the main position at the moment. And everything points to that position being retained and intensified. In 1921 there were 134 distilleries at work in Scotland. In 1933 there were 15 (including 6 patent stills). Last year the number of pot stills at work had increased again. But the future of Highland malt whisky, other than as a flavouring ingredient of patent spirit, is very obscure.

*   *   *

That is a pity because the general prospect stands not for temperance or other ideal but for adulteration and degradation, for the vicious monkey and the banner of Red Biddy. Each pot still might very well carry as proud a name as any one of the vineyards of France. The aim should be quality above all else, a perfect matured spirit, whose aroma and flavour would be distinctive without ever being harsh, whose essential oils would impart a gentle glowing warmth throughout the body, a delicate excitement and fine clarity to the brain. What, it might be asked, is the final difference between a perfect wine and a perfect whisky? I was about to answer that wine is intricately of the body and whisky of the mind; but that would not be obviously true, for whisky warms the body more quickly than wine and wine has its elevating influence on the mind; yet —and this is possibly my contention—the effect of the wine in both spheres is more sensuous. On the last pinnacle, where wine moves to the colour and cadence of language, whisky moves to its ultimate meaning. Though I see, even as I write, that such distinctions are impossible, if not absurd, yet in some obstinate way I am left aware that what I say is true. Whisky is concerned about the limitations of the mind; it is masculine and penetrative. It can be coarse and aggressive. But, perfectly conceived, it is creative fire. On the other hand, wine . . . what a sudden light comes flooding the ancient conjunction: wine and women!

To get whisky of true quality, the public would have to know about it and demand it. Its flavour would have to be understood and appreciated. A devotee of fortified Empire wines would spit forth a delicate light wine of France as watery and insipid. The Cockney child from his slum on a first visit to the country could not eat a fresh egg because ' it ain't got no taste, lady.'

Perfect knowledge and appreciation beget natural temperance. A palate used to the best will deny itself rather than suffer debauch from the worst.

A glimpse of this natural temperance we got a little earlier in these pages when discussing certain statutes imposed on the Isles early in the seventeenth century. A still was a normal household possession and apparently caused no drunkenness or breach of the peace. We may start up aghast at the thought of a ' common man ' having a free still in his house to-day. I can imagine ardent ' temperance reformers ' looking upon the thought—and upon me—as inspired by the Devil. Yet the simple truth is that many wealthy business and professional men—not to mention, of course, Galsworthian Tories of the purpler vintages—have cellars containing whiskies and wines capable of keeping themselves and their families in perpetual befuddlement for a generation. Do we think of such incontinence amongst them? On the contrary, most of us know that their wines, like their pictures or household appointments, are as fine as they can get them, and that they represent not potential private drunkenness but a highly social, temperate, and rather charming way of living. We recognize this, and many envy or aspire to it. What profound snobbery, then, to stand aghast at the thought of the ' common man ' having similar privilege! How debased I, as a common man, must have become that social or liquor reformers should foam at the mouth at the thought of my being able to drink what I wanted! How great the superiority on their part!

Yet there is this in it: their self-righteous fury is an index of the social degradation of the common man, of his loss of natural dignity. Having debauched and herded him, the ruling powers must make sure that the natural appetites which they have perverted must be finally denied.

The old Gael made his own whisky and retained his natural dignity: exceeding in this even the Galsworthian squire who though he had the dignity could make nothing.

And according to Martin, as I have already pointed out, he made at least three kinds or degrees of whisky, the last, usquebaugh-baul being four times distilled and therefore very strong. We have earlier records of the same thing in Ireland. Theoricus, praising aqua-vitae to ' the ninth degree ' (as an Elizabethan put it), distinguished these three kinds as simplex, composita, and perfectissima. It is recorded, too, that flavouring herbs were used. With usquebaugh-baul and herbs (of which the Gael's knowledge was extensive, particularly for medicinal purposes and dyes), they must have made some remarkable liqueurs, and undoubtedly have inspired, if not actually compounded, the finer of those we buy to-day. This may seem a large claim, but we know that in Europe the Celts were the first in the field with distilling, that they made a strong and therefore very pure spirit capable of being variously flavoured, that it was so flavoured, and that the scholars of the early Celtic church were missionaries on the Continent. Indeed the Gaelic word *lusadh*, drinking, is derived from *lus*, a herb or plant.

My main difficulty for olden times lies in this matter of maturing. As far as can be gathered, they did not store their uisgebeatha in order to let time mellow it. Although here, to be just, we are up against imperfect knowledge—and I personally am sceptical. In *The Scottish Gael*, Logan writes: ' The making of butter produces whey, a wholesome liquor, which some of the Highlanders, Buchanan says, boiled and kept under ground for several months, by which it was rendered a very agreeable beverage.' To ask me to believe that a folk who had discovered this about whey had not discovered it about whisky is to strain credulity to smiling point. In the smuggling times we know they drank it new. But furtiveness—and therefore a certain debauch—had crept in by that time. The smugglers were hunted folk. Volumes could easily be filled with ' smuggling stories ' : but they all have the same motif, are essentially of the same pattern. In one sense they stand for adventure; in another, for an undoubted deterioration in dignity. The forces of law and order appeared to them to have been wrongly and unnaturally directed, but they were forces that had to be cunningly evaded. Alasdair of Kiltarlity, that kind godly man, it will be remembered, had to take his whisky to the inn at midnight concealed in a cartload of peats. But there are one or two points in that simple story worth perhaps special notice. He had to sell the whisky he had made from his own barley in order *to pay his rent*. It was the screw of the landlord, the chief; and during the infamous times of the ' clearances,' great chiefs actually used it as an excuse for turning the people out of their homes, in order to get bigger rents from sheep-farmers. Next, Alasdair always prayed to God to keep him from being officially detected. And thirdly, having arrived before the inn at midnight—to find the officer waiting, Alasdair blamed God for having betrayed him; but it was not God who had betrayed Alasdair, *it was the publican*.

Now I did not give the whole story in an earlier page. As Alasdair blamed God, the officer was aware of simple sincerity. So he told Alasdair to go in and deliver the goods and collect his dues. This Alasdair did; then the officer entered the inn and seized the illicit spirit, while Alasdair went on his way, doubtless greatly troubled in thought over his God, his chief, and his publican—and this alien force that had so unexpectedly exercised such clemency.

Among the papers in the charter-room of Blair Castle is a petition from tenants in Strathtummel, dated 1848, pointing out that the ' Petitioners had hitherto struggled hard to pay their rents, not out of their small holdings, that being impossible, but in a way (which although looked upon by some as a breach of law and propriety, yet was looked upon by the petitioners in a different way) which they begged to inform His Grace of, viz.: that of illicit distillation, whereby during the time the petitioners were not entirely prevented, they and each of them managed from what was not required for the use of the family to turn out of their barley sufficient means to pay their rent.' Despite failure of the potato crop and other ills, they might still manage to pay their rents if ' His Grace's assistance could be so managed that the stringency of the excise laws as against them could be although only partially removed. The petitioners did not want any legislative enactment for accomplishing this, the mere removal of the District officer . . . would . . . be sufficient.'

The ancient social goodness of the commune or township, when a man could make his own drink out of his own barley, is already deep in the toils of evasion and fear though still capable of exhibiting a charming naïveté!

Altogether Alasdair's adventure is pretty much the parable of what whisky has meant to the Highlands— and, in the larger social sense, to the whole of Scotland.

Even the whisky that is being made by smugglers to-day would appear no longer to be produced from barley but from the molasses bought as feeding stuff for their cattle.

Yet at no time in the whole history of distilling has there existed finer whisky than now lies in the ware-houses of our Highland stills. The true whisky is not a legend, any more than the true Scotland. But the amount of natural and social reorganization required to give Alasdair of Kiltarlity his dignity and his dram is enough to dishearten even an ardent Nationalist! A work of Hercules? A work for Finn and his whole company of sleepers! A work for ourselves—*sinn fein*, in the Gaelic tongue : two simple words, but sufficient to swell the ranks of the teetotallers against me with a rare blend of socialist internationalists, Tory clubmen, and aspiring Clissolds. Listening acutely, one may hear them hissing—patent spirit, soda, and carbonic acid (respectively). Truly this is anything but being discreet! Yet my intentions are so simple: to cultivate our tastes and our barley patches, with reason and the help of science, so that we may enrich ourselves and the world. But ourselves first—in decency, in modesty. With publican's whisky what it can be, how may I tell a Slav to weaken his vodka or a Teuton to put less gas in his beer? If we cut off the output of blatancy and carbonic acid, science and manners could put the world right in a week. Some day some small country may show how to set about it. I should like to think I knew the name of that country!

SOME SINGLE WHISKIES

I<small>T</small> is high time that something was said, by way of appreciation or discrimination, of some of the pot-still whiskies. Yet though here at last I should be prepared to rush in, actually I am aware of an extreme diffidence, for I know that pot stills with a very indifferent reputation as single or self-whiskies have had their perfect periods, and famous names out of the Glenlivet country and elsewhere can definitely on occasion be 'not so good.' When I hesitated— as I did—over including the section dealing with the manufacture of pot spirit, what drove me to it was this need to make plain the difficulty of achieving a perfect uniformity in the product of any individual still not merely from season to season but from week to week, even from cask to cask. I do not wish to exaggerate this uncertainty, noticeable only occasionally to cultivated palates, yet it is liable to be there, and when it comes to the invidious business of selecting Highland distilleries for special comment, I begin to wonder how to start! Perhaps also I am trying to suggest to a reader who may be moved by these notes to the adventure of discovering a self-whisky for himself, two things: that each pot still has its own characteristics, and accordingly a purchase of one bottle of a single whisky is an insufficient test of all the stills; and that, as in the case of great art, immediate appreciation may not be the general rule.

Let me risk illustrating this. In his *Notes on a Cellar Book*, Saintsbury says he used to keep Clynelish, Smith's Glenlivet, Glen Grant, Talisker, Glendronach, and one of the Islay brands—Lagavulin, Ardbeg, Coal Isla, etc. (Of the Campbelltown whiskies, by the way, he says nothing, though in his day some twenty distilleries must have been at work there. These whiskies, as a matter of fact, have gone completely out of favour with the blenders, and as the blenders rule the whisky industry, this area is now practically derelict. A sad business.)

These names mentioned by Saintsbury had in his day a popular reputation. And as he would be the last man to praise what he had not first tasted and found good, we may conclude that in this case he happily endorsed prevailing tradition. Yet what names he omitted! Deliberately mentioning his selection to an old distiller the other day (whose still was not included), I received the comment, very dry, 'That was the usual list.' (This distiller had actually a pleasant recollection of Saintsbury by whom

he had been, in Elgin, specially coached in Latin.)
To come to my point: a short time ago I spent an
hour or two with a northern merchant who was
making up his private blend, in which two of the
above whiskies were included. There were samples
from other pot stills. Of them all, as it happened,
that which appealed to me as the most perfectly
palatable came from an Inverness distillery (Glen
Mhor). And I mention it here for one particular
reason: there was no slightest trace of that ' guff '
which so often repels the palate used to the dead
smoothness of a silent spirit. Indeed it may be said
that until a man has had the luck to chance upon a
perfectly matured well-mannered whisky, he does not
really know what whisky is.

There are many distilleries in the north capable of
producing this fine self-whisky. But I admit, as
things are, they may be a bit difficult to come by.
At the moment I know of only two pot stills that
bottle on their own premises: Glenfiddich and
Strathisla. Many of the other malts are bottled by
merchants, but naturally the great blenders do not
look with favour on such competition. Even distilleries owned by private individuals or companies
hardly dare go into a bottling business on their own
premises, lest orders from the blenders for new whisky
might altogether cease.

How can this state of affairs be altered? Only, I am afraid, by such a demand on the part of the public for a single whisky as will inspire distillers to meet it.

A single whisky suitable to their taste can be got by those genuinely concerned to find it. I have mentioned Glenfiddich and Strathisla as being bottled by private distillers. They are both very sound whiskies, the true Speyside flavour requiring perhaps a slight cultivation by what I may call a 'silent' palate. There are many others bottled by merchants in the course of their private business (some of our northern whisky merchants lay down casks yearly at several pot stills), such as Glen Grant, The Glenlivet, Talisker, Glenmorangie, Dalmore, Glenburgie, Linkwood, Pulteney, Highland Park, etc. Glen Grant, bottled by a firm in Elgin, carries a label 'matured in sherry wood for ten years.' The other week in Edinburgh, I came across a Glen Grant bottled by Mackinlays & Co., Leith, that was really very fine. This is a whisky with a reputation to maintain. It is full-bodied and of fairly uniform quality. In certain circumstances it might be found a trifle penetrating to untried palates, but that is a matter to deliberate thoughtfully. Smith's Glenlivet in my youth used to share premier honours with Glen Grant. Historically speaking, Glenlivet is a synonym for 'the real stuff.' It has much literary anecdote attached to it. Often have I listened to the differing points of view regarding the famous law suit by which Smith's Glenlivet attempted to secure exclusive use of the word Glenlivet and failed, but the real story may not be retailed here. Talisker at its best can be superb, but I have known it adopt the uncertain manners of Skye weather. I have two or three pleasant memories of it, however; one, in particular, concerning an ex-president of the Alpine Club who used to come to Skye for the Cuillin and fishing. I happened to gather that he had once travelled across Europe to greet a few magnums of a champagne deemed to have been exhausted. We were staying in the same little hotel, where I had happily been presented with a special bottle of Talisker, and I had the very considerable pleasure of watching a meeting between two spirits perfectly matched.

Glenmorangie always seemed to me rather a delicate whisky, quite lacking in coarseness, and capable of maturing fairly early. Though I have not tasted it now for some years, it suggests to my mind the qualities of an immediately palatable whisky. I had an interesting experience with Dalmore in Invergordon (where it is now bottled) just after the war, when I happened to drop into a little ' school ' who ordered nine gallons at a time direct from the distillery (a distiller's licence does not permit of a sale of less than nine gallons). Though it was not so old as it might have been, it certainly sustained its reputation; an all-round reliable whisky, capable in its best moods, I should say, of a pronounced excellence: a remark that may equally be applied to Linkwood, Glenburgie, Ord, Millburn, and many another. I mention these names deliberately because I have recently seen them bottled and for sale as single whiskies. I must say something of Pulteney—the whisky of my native county—Old Pulteney, as it was always called, though I have childhood memories of seeing it in bottle perfectly white and certainly new. In those days it was potent stuff, consumed, I should say, on the quays of Wick more for its effect than its flavour! A very individual whisky, it was naturally disliked by some as ardently as it was praised by others. Whisky has its human parallel. It is not a machine-made article and has to be come upon as one comes upon a friend, and then treated with proper respect. When I got of an age to understand Old Pulteney, I could admire its quality when well matured, recognizing in it some of the strong characteristics of the northern temperament. Though very pronounced in flavour, it was never quite so peaty as some of the Speyside stills, which occasionally err just a trifle in this respect, I think. I have not yet visited Highland Park in the Orkneys though I have tasted sound samples of it a few times. Again, like Pulteney, it is a full-flavoured whisky out of a stern strong environment, yet I can very well believe the story of a friend of mine who was once presented with two bottles by the owner of the still and doled out thimblefuls of the mellowed power on odd occasions to the intimate and discerning.

I have always observed, by the way, a singular benevolence and generosity in those who appreciate (and therefore rarely abuse) the finer moods of spirits and wines. And even for those who may appreciate too deeply and too often, what a benevolence is aroused in us! This friend, who is an Englishman with an almost exhaustive knowledge of single whiskies, illustrated very well this matter of pronounced flavour one day we were discussing the Islay stills. 'Leaning against the wind and rain, you drive off from the first tee at Machrie. You feel your ball has gone straight, so with head down you plod on. . . . Eighteen holes of that—and then a glass of Lagavulin! It's not that it revives you: it crawls along to your finger-tips and toe-nails in a divine glow. . . . But if I had been golfing in a hot sun at Eastbourne— would I have been looking forward to this potent stuff at the end?'

Probably not. The usual blend with a dash of soda would doubtless have been ordered! Yet when we seriously began to discuss the matter we came to one very important—and what will seem to many a very astonishing—conclusion, drawn from a wide range of evidence, namely, that though a blended whisky, containing a large proportion of patent spirit, may *seem* lighter and taste lighter than a malt whisky, in actuality its subsequent effect is less pleasant —another way, after all, of expressing the monkey story! The idea, in other words, that a pure pot-still whisky is heavier and ' more headachy ' than the customary blend is a popular myth—the reverse normally being true. But it is an understandable myth, because tastelessness is desired by those who need the stimulus of straight alcohol, either from physical weakness or lack of palate.

These generous whiskies, with their individual flavours, do recall the world of hills and glens, of raging elements, of shelter, of divine ease. The perfect moment for their reception is after arduous bodily stress—or mental stress, if the body be sound. The essential oils that wind in the glass then uncurl their long fingers in lingering benediction and the nobler works of Creation are made manifest. At such a moment, the basest man would bless his enemy. And so, convoluting like the oils, we come back to the conception not of conquering but of civilizing!

But much will have to be done by the pot stills

of the Highlands before their virtues may be widely appreciated. A whisky produced with too strong a flavour to meet the blender's needs will have to modify its manners for private company. That is a difficult problem, I know, because it involves the basic question of economic existence. Again, each still would have to strive to maintain its own character with as uniform an excellence as possible. This would mean extreme care in production with the main aim quality rather than quantity. There is still some room for research here and for experiment in the way of vatting carefully selected parcels of whisky on the distillery premises. Saintsbury mentions very favourably a blend he made of Glen Grant and Talisker. But such blending of different single whiskies may be carried out by merchants, not by distillers, and, anyway, is a secondary consideration and one that does not unduly rouse my enthusiasm. I have never yet met any blend of all malts or of malt and patent that had the individuality and distinction of a perfect sample of single whisky. The single whisky is the heart of our problem, as it is the foundation of the whole whisky trade, Combine and all. The great pity is that it should have been deflected to the business of flavouring patent spirit instead of to a natural growth within itself, a growth that the Government of this country could have protected and assisted both at home and abroad (by international agreement) as Portugal so sucessfully has done with her port. I am aware it sounds a trifle fantastic to think of a Westminster Government doing anything that would even allow the Highlands to help themselves: it is so much easier to maintain the popular and picturesque notion of poverty and charity—while continuing to collect an annual revenue of millions of pounds from what was first brewed by the Highlander in his pot still as uisgebeatha.

AN ECONOMIC NOTE

THE Highlands have had, of course, that romantic past to which some of us refer only with reluctance. The 'clearances' of the early nineteenth century, when vast numbers of the crofters were driven from their homes, often in circumstances of extreme brutality, mark perhaps a high spot in that long process of decline that is the underlying theme of the historic story in modern times. Altogether it is a disheartening story in a disheartened people, losing faith in themselves, growing ashamed of their Gaelic speech, of every characteristic that differentiated them from those born to the English tongue. The world had conquered them, a bright world before which simplicity and poverty were secret sins. What really defeated them was their own sensitiveness, out of a past concerned for those things of the mind natural to good breeding. Not that it all happened in a state of continuous gloom. The Celtic people love variety and witty sayings and fun. But it did become common for southern visitors to talk of evasiveness, of deceit, of two faces, and, more searchingly, ' The Highlander will tell you a lie rather than hurt your feelings.' It was all in the air, the air that passed so refreshingly over heather hills, but bore to the senses now and then the faint carrion smell of the dead eagle trapped by the gamekeepers.

That phase has almost passed and now we have what we may call the strutters—those who parade the tartan at fashionable assemblies and mods with an air of esoteric knowledge and exclusive privilege, but who would be horrified at mention of the word politics in connection with their own land. They make their money in ' the other world.'

That tawdry, slightly shameful phase will pass also, and presently the ordinary Highlander, who has forgotten most of his Gaelic and has never worn a kilt, aware of the unspeakable slum life—something more desperate than he has ever known—that is the real stomach of the conqueror, will begin to demand less glamour and more barley, less intoxication by windy rhetoric and more by the true water of life.

He will demand to know — for our uisgebeatha wasn't far away !—why his whisky should be so heavily taxed compared with other drinks. People in the south of England make their own cider out of their own apples and consume it without paying a farthing in duty (happy people! I would suggest to them a revolution before they give up that privilege), yet if

WHISKY

cider were taxed on the same alcoholic basis as whisky
it would have to pay a duty of 6s. 5d. a gallon. We
have seen that colonial wine pays 4s. a gallon when
on the same basis as whisky it should pay over 30s.
Foreign wines at 65 under proof pay 8s. instead of
over 25s. While beer, the English national brew and
drink, is taxed at just about half the whisky rate.
And over and above all that, whisky, by law, must
be kept three years before it is used, with consequent
overhead charges and loss in bulk. Actually very little
pot-still whisky reaches the market under five years
old; while the stocks that have been accumulating
through continuous decline in consumption, owing to
the excessive duty, point to an average age for some
time to come of nearer seven years.

This discrimination against whisky is so manifestly
unjust that it does have the appearance of being
deliberately vindictive. If the ends of temperance or
teetotalism were being attained, certain minds might
feel justified. But, as we have seen, they are not.
If any end at all is being attained it is that of changing
the good-natured to the vicious! If the Chancellor
of the Exchequer says he is not concerned with
temperance but with revenue, then he is doing his
utmost to defeat his purpose as the decline in receipts
since 1920 (when the duty was raised to 72s. 6d.
a proof gallon) shows. In 1920 the revenue from

spirits was 58 million pounds; in 1934 it was 33 millions.

No foreign country behaves in this manner to a native product. The whole idea of a tariff is to protect the home article against the foreign. In every other country they so protect and foster their native drinks. But in this country we deliberately lure the foreigner to destroy Scotch whisky.

But perhaps to our Government a Scottish product *is* a foreign product! A sudden illumination that explains much—though I can hardly believe it! No, the whole thing must be meaningless—if possibly (let credit be given) in the pure abstract sense of certain modern art. We all know how capable our Westminster politicians are of really superb efforts in the irrational.

At its lowest this is a plea against the deceit and humbug and adulteration and degradation that attend on drinking. If alcohol is bad for us, let us cut it off altogether. If we cannot trust ourselves to take or leave a thing, let us destroy it utterly. All that we have done by our laws in this matter of alcohol is to ensure that it shall be got by the common people of our country in as cheap and nasty a condition as possible—during prescribed hours! If there is any satisfaction in the destroying of a people's taste, and therefore of their self-respect, and consequently of their sobriety, I submit it savours less of the irrational than of the diabolic.

In France, where restrictive legislation is at a minimum, sobriety is the rule. Indeed drunkenness in that country is regarded pretty much as sexual immorality is in this; yet the consumption per head of alcohol in France is three times what it is in Britain. I refer to alcohol in distilled spirits, not to wine of which the consumption is at least fifty times greater than in our country. (Though let it be recorded that staunch England comes to our rescue to bowl them out on beer!) Yet I have tried—but lamentably failed—to visualize M. Crémieux in a wild rush for alcohol and wine. Let me quote him again, in view of the above facts (taken from evidence led before the 1930 Licensing Commission): 'This violent taste for alcohol which begins beyond the frontiers of France always remains rather mysterious to a Frenchman from south of the Loire, where people drink brandy and *fine champagne* much as they smell a flower. But the harshness of the climate no doubt explains the use and abuse of strong drink.' There is something so noble in the humanity of this utterance that being a Highlander I am prepared to blame our climate rather than hurt anyone's feelings.

The old Scots, Boece recorded, were moderate drinkers. But then in his day they could brew and drink as much as they liked. 'The Highlanders,' wrote Logan, 'can enjoy a social glass as much as any person; but although whisky is plentiful with them, habitual tippling is extremely rare and there is a proverb which speaks their contempt of those who meet for the sake of drinking only. The renowned Fingal, who, by the bye, delivered his maxims in Triads, said, that one of the worst things which could happen to a man was to drink curmi in the morning.' (Curmi = ale.) All of which is interesting, coming out of that land which was so 'stark opposite' to any semblance of civilization. Clearly Fingal and M. Crémieux would have hit it off very well together (without needlessly diminishing their consumption per head).

For the rest, the American experiment proved that you cannot legislate a people into sobriety—whatever else the effort may do. The reform in our drinking habits in recent generations has been the result of a change in social habits—particularly the social habits of our wealthy or landed classes who were the real drunkards, and who manifestly could still get drunk despite the duty. As for the poor, the wretched squalor of the slums in a new uncomprehended utterly soulless industrial world drove them, as we have seen, to seek forgetfulness in drink; is doing so to this day to an accompaniment of gangs and bottle-slashing, but more and more with an inbred viciousness that can be roused *without drink*. The Labour Party has Temperance as one of its ' planks.' That it is merely a cunning plank is its miserable weakness, for it shows the lack of great leadership and action, of a passionate generosity that has no time for planks and dodges on its way to the realization of social decency and freedom. Better that the vision without which we perish be kept alive on whisky than not kept alive at all!

Now I admit when I first mentioned the Highlands, I was really thinking of the fisherman, the crofter, the shepherd, of his environment, with its distances and play of elemental forces, the long strenuous months when a pot of beer lies in his belly cold as death by drowning and cider is an affair of solemn eructation. As for the lighter French wines—I know he can always, of course, reserve these until he returns home in the evening in time to change for dinner.

*   *   *

The purely economic aspect of the manufacture of whisky is of very definite importance to Scotland. A conservative estimate gives the average pot still during its working season a consumption of some 4000 quarters of barley and 500 tons of coal. In the year 1929 with eighty odd pot stills at work it was reckoned that over 400,000 quarters of barley were used at a total price of £935,000 (1930 Licensing Commission Report). If one contemplated not merely all the pot stills at work but pot-still whisky really coming into its own, then Highland agriculture would flourish forever! Employment is given directly and indirectly to thousands of workers. Industries of many kinds, from transport to coopering, are freshly stimulated. New industry would arise. For example, in damp seasons, home barley should be dried on a kiln, but how can farmers or distillers arrange for the erection of the necessary plant, when they hardly know from year to year whether a hundred stills are to be at work or ten? The sale or non-sale of his barley makes too often all the difference between solvency and insolvency to the northern farmer.

Last year the Exchequer drew from the consumption of Scotch whisky in Britain some £30,000,000, well over two-thirds of the total amount spent on all national services in Scotland.

However, this is neither a trade nor a political pamphlet and the implications of figures can look after themselves. What I am trying to bring out is that here we have an industry which could offset by export, if fairly dealt with and properly organized, much of the import of luxuries that have become normal to our civilized condition, internally assist agriculture and give well-paid employment, while raising from a reasonable duty a very considerable sum towards the running of the State. Such duty should certainly not exceed 14s. 9d. a proof gallon—the figure it stood at in 1914. (The present fantastic figure is 72s. 6d. a proof gallon.) The minimum age for consumption might well be raised to five years. Whisky would then still be a very dear drink.

The Highlander—the Scot—does not want to be a beggar. He does not like to be told that he is not paying his way like an Englishman. He is beginning to feel that the exploitation of his whisky is a parable for the exploitation of much else. One day he may wake up and in the face of so much conquering decide that some civilizing (despite Mr Buchan) is at last due an innings.

★ ★ ★

But, it may be asked, even if our sordid economic squabbles and international bad manners were mended, would not so barren a region as the Highlands be inevitably left derelict? The rest of Scotland with its perfect balance of industry and agriculture might make shift to look after itself, but the Highlands—what could ever be there, beyond various wild birds and beasts for amiable slaughter in Society's season, and for sportsmen's reminiscences concerning the same, complete with photographs of the gillie who could distinguish the heel of a flask without spectacles at 95 years?

Yet how naturally rich this Highland region is, what potential wealth dumbly awaits creation! Inexhaustible resources of hydro-electric power, great areas for afforestation and stock-raising, a vast fishing industry—the great Scottish herring-fishing ports are all north of the Highland line, sea-inlets opening into glens where timber-working, weaving, fish-curing, etc., should be communal industries. . . . But what I really want to stress is the quality of the natural products: the best mutton and meat in the world, the finest game and salmon and trout, white fish of unexcelled firmness and flavour, herring that are admittedly the pick of all markets (the Norwegian are coarse in comparison), fragrant berries, heather honey (on a vast scale) of so exquisite a flavour that a world grown economically sane could never have enough of it, and—did I mention whisky? Ancient records refer to Scotland as a land flowing with milk and honey—a literal reference to the extensive herds and cottage bee-hives of a once happy folk.

Surely, too, the utmost practical use of science could be made by a people who have a world reputation as engineers. If Mr Dunne can mathematically prove the immortality of the mind from a study of what the Highlander calls second-sight, is it too much to hope that an intensive exploration of witchcraft (one of our older Scottish industries) might not result in a knowledge of raising the wind? And to command the winds might very well be to command the clouds. Think of the orders from the parched regions of the world! *Timbuctoo radiogram: Please despatch four cumulus clouds, Fort William origin, by first wind on Monday.* The Highlands could spare a few rain clouds and still leave some water in Loch Ness. There would at least be one purely humanitarian benefit in this cloud traffic: we would be given an opportunity of explaining that the only thing a man of taste adds to whisky is water. And when I use the word whisky I can but hope that the reader who has followed this long and devious excursion may now have some faint glimmering of what I mean. I wish him (and her) the best, anyway!